EMERALD WOUNDS

Praise for *Emerald Wounds* by Joyce Mansour

"Slippery, stained, and gloriously indelicate, Joyce Mansour reveals to us the grisly face of eros."

—ELAINE KAHN, AUTHOR OF *WOMEN IN PUBLIC*

"It is high time (and way past it!) that someone bring to publishing daylight the truly great range of poems by the English/Egyptian writer/artist/entertainer Joyce Patricia Adès, whom we salute as Joyce Mansour. Emilie Moorhouse has just accomplished this feat and we can gladly say, to this bilingual and welcome presentation of a large selection of those texts with City Lights, a very loud hooray!"

—MARY ANN CAWS, AUTHOR OF *SYMBOLISM, DADA, SURREALISM: SELECTED ESSAYS*

"'I love, Madame, the scent of black orchids—ultra-black—of your poems,' wrote André Breton when he received Joyce Mansour's first book, *Screams* (*Cris*, 1953), with her dedication, 'These few screams, en hommage.' This legendary Surrealist woman poet with her singular lyric fusion of love and death, phantasies of gleeful and grim inexorability, constructs radical strategies of irrational disjunction. Rich with ancient ritual and story from her Egyptian Jewish heritage, Mansour's impetuous sprints at times become marathons. Elegant and raw, the impulsive, dramatic energy of eros excites the activity of language with pressured, passionate diction, writing as act of possession through the sonic matter of words. Like early Arabic poets, speaking not only for themselves but to and about themselves, Mansour can shift the poet's identity by her use of pronouns 'with your mouth for a pillow.' Then again, her erotic haunts have immediate impact—'I want to be naked in your singing eyes.' Translated with verve by Emilie Moorhouse."

—NORMA COLE, AUTHOR OF *FATE NEWS*

"Fierce, uncompromising, intelligent, weird, assertive, abject—Joyce Mansour's poems are a long cry of female rage and desire. The world is 'a shitting bird,' the dead 'bloom like Parma hams,' and the patriarchy subverted, mocked, and challenged at every turn, in personal relationships with men, in the fatuous advice of women's magazines. 'I do not know hell,' Mansour writes, 'But my body has been burning ever since I was born.' These poems are the searing result of that life."

—KIM ADDONIZIO, AUTHOR OF *NOW WE'RE GETTING SOMEWHERE*

"Among the many dark pleasures of *Emerald Wounds*, most marvelous is Joyce Mansour's canny adaptation of the Surrealist impulse towards revolt to subversively femme ends. In Emilie Moorhouse's astonishingly fresh translations, these palm-sized poems are arousing, alarming, and, finally, transformational, offering outlandish anti-psalms, sex tips from the devil, adroit instruction manuals for surviving the eradicating world. Like emeralds held so tightly they bite the flesh, these poems are compressed, brilliant works of maximum refulgence."

—JOYELLE MCSWEENEY, AUTHOR OF *TOXICON AND ARACHNE*

"Transgressive delight and terror of the supreme surreal feminist in this remarkable and most original book of dreams. Mansour, 'an animal of the night,' has been waiting to be reclaimed and counted. She who 'prunes the sky with carnivorous thighs,' whose ruse lies in a chignon, is wonderfully abetted in these excellent, luminous translations. A poet who listens to the 'dialect of undressed sexes' and 'pierces the stagnant eye of the night' is the aligning, yet jolting force we've all been anticipating. This is her moment."

—ANNE WALDMAN, AUTHOR OF *BARD, KINETIC*

"In Joyce Mansour's exuberant, macabre, strange and sexy poems, I find such kinship, such lineage, such permission. It is such a delight to read this collection and meet her. These poems invite me to be brave, to be loud, to cackle and mourn and seduce. I only wish we'd met sooner, that I'd known sooner to place myself in her lineage."

—SAFIA ELHILLO, AUTHOR OF *GIRLS THAT NEVER DIE*

"In the poetry of Joyce Mansour, we feel the churn of the devouring and excreting body and its parts. Each part emits parts: the lover births his sex; the receptive octopus outputs its legs like a burst seedpod. Vicious as childbirth, delicate as the tension in a throat about to speak, Mansour's poems demand we attend to the forbidden maximums of our desires."

—SOPHIA DAHLIN, AUTHOR OF *NATCH*

"*Emerald Wounds* feels like a resuscitation. Joyce Mansour's Arab Jewish consciousness sticks its tongue out in the face of macho Euro mores. Given new breath by translator Emilie Moorhouse, Mansour's work is phantastic, inverted, explicit, full of spells. It seems to predict and override the world's weakening lust, calling out from a past of feverish slits, Sekhmet and the joy of piss."

—TAMARA FAITH BERGER, AUTHOR OF *MAIDENHEAD*

EMERALD WOUNDS

SELECTED POEMS OF

JOYCE MANSOUR

translated by Emilie Moorhouse

edited by Emilie Moorhouse and Garrett Caples

CITY LIGHTS | SAN FRANCISCO

Library of Congress Cataloging-in-Publication Data
Names: Mansour, Joyce, 1928–1986, author. | Moorhouse, Emilie, writer of foreword, translator, editor. | Caples, Garrett T., editor.
Title: Emerald wounds : selected poems of Joyce Mansour / Joyce Mansour ; foreword by Emilie Moorhouse ; translated by Emilie Moorhouse ; edited by Emilie Moorhouse and Garrett Caples.
Description: San Francisco, CA : City Lights Books, 2023.
Identifiers: LCCN 2022054291 | ISBN 9780872869011 (paperback)
Subjects: LCGFT: Poetry.
Classification: LCC PQ2673.A5 E64 2023 | DDC 841/.914—dc23/
    eng/20221222
LC record available at https://lccn.loc.gov/2022054291

City Lights Books are published at the City Lights Bookstore,
261 Columbus Avenue, San Francisco, CA 94133

www.citylights.com

TABLE OF CONTENTS

POEMS FROM *BIEF* (1958–1960)

RAPACES (1960) / BIRDS OF PREY

CARRÉ BLANC (1965) / WHITE SQUARE

I : "OÙ LE BAS BLESSE" / I: "WHERE THE SHOE HURTS"

Translating Desire: The Erotic-Macabre Poetry of Joyce Mansour

Emilie Moorhouse

In 1966, the first English-language account of the desire-filled poems of cigar-smoking Egyptian surrealist Joyce Mansour appeared, perhaps fittingly, in the section of the journal *Books Abroad* called "Not in the Reviews."[1] In this article, "The Poetry of Joyce Mansour," pioneering British scholar of surrealism J. H. Matthews laments Mansour's lack of recognition from literary critics, who seemed intent on ignoring her. Even today, a half-century later, Joyce Mansour's work remains underappreciated in France and virtually unknown in the rest of the world. Given the entrenched sexism of literary circles, the fact that a woman's shameless and provocative writing on sex and death—what Matthews terms her "cries of uninhibited desire"—has been shunned by the literary establishment for so long is hardly a surprise.

In the fall of 2017, I was looking for poems in preparation for a literary translation workshop. A few days after I began my search, the #MeToo movement went viral, putting a new spotlight on sexism and the abuse of power in our cultural industries. What I found most striking among the ugly stories of assault, harassment, silencing, and coercion that were breaking on a daily basis was the extent to which our culture continually dismisses and denies the needs and desires of women, while centering the importance of male desire in so many narratives.

I set new parameters on my search: I decided I needed to translate the writing of a woman who spoke openly and shamelessly about her desires. I

1

knew that, as I looked further back in time, almost any woman who spoke her truth was likely to have been ignored, forgotten, dismissed, or worse. After all, if so many prominent women were experiencing abuse and silencing in 2017, how many prior works of art by women were relegated to the dark corners of history? Without a doubt, there were works that had been shelved and forgotten for the sole reason that they had been held to different standards than those written by men; women's writing has often been judged as "too much": too sultry, too frigid, too hysterical. If the pre-2017 world had not been ready for these voices, perhaps we had finally reached a moment where our culture could embrace them.

France, of course, has experienced periods of exceptional openness in publishing that benefited women writers; French-Canadian poet Anne Hébert, for example, moved to Paris in 1954 when her work was considered too dark by Canadian publishers, who embraced Leonard Cohen's brooding poetry only a few years later. Yet French culture also remained fiercely loyal to its romanticized ideas of female submission and male domination. This dichotomy meant that, while certain controversial literary female authors were indeed published—such as Renée Vivien, an openly lesbian British poet who wrote passionate love poems in French at the turn of the 20th century—women's voices were still subjugated or eclipsed by those of men. Such was the perceived misogyny of France's highest literary award, le Prix Goncourt, that in 1904, a year after its creation, 22 literary women launched an alternate prize, le Prix Femina, awarded by an all-female jury. To this day, the jury for the Prix Goncourt hasn't taken the hint: A mere 13 women have received the prize since it was created.

It was in this context that I came across the poems of Joyce Mansour, born Joyce Patricia Adès (1928–1986). Her work is defiant; even by today's standards, it smashes taboos around female expression and desire. Like her poetry, Mansour's life is fascinating. Born in England in 1928, she was raised in Cairo in a wealthy, cosmopolitan family of Jewish-Syrian descent. Early on, she experienced two tragedies that would haunt the rest of her life: When she was 15, her mother died of cancer. The teenager was deeply affected by this loss; although surrounded by a loving father and siblings, she was inconsolable. As an escape from her grief, she immersed herself in the world of sports, where she excelled at the long jump and sprinting. As she began to slowly find meaning in her life again, she met and fell in love with a young athletic man, Henri Naggar. The two formed a perfect couple who seemed to have everything life could offer: youth, good looks, and wealthy families. They could only have a bright future ahead and were married when she was 18 and he 21. But only six months after their wedding, following a long honeymoon during which they traveled through Europe, Naggar died very suddenly of cancer.[2]

This second loss was almost too much for her to bear. She locked herself away, refusing to see anyone, even her father, and suffering from night terrors and sleepwalking. She cut herself off from her friends, accepting only the company of her sister-in-law, whom she stayed with. It was during this time she began composing poetry. Plunged into a deep depression, she turned to poetry as a way to cope and "remove the blood from [her] dreams."[3] Her very first lines were "Improvised poems in the bathtub. Alone, she would talk, scream as though to cover the sound of the water. It was a kind of revolt."[4] Mansour's earliest poems were composed in English, and she later described them as "Crazed with rage . . . exclusively insults . . . In fact, no one has ever seen them." Indeed, none of these poems have ever been found.

As such origins suggest, Mansour's poetry lies at the opposite end of the spectrum from the concept of art for art's sake. For her, aestheticism in poetry expresses nothing. She described poetry as "a scream," illustrating her assertion with the following anecdote: "I went to the cemetery for a Muslim funeral. Suddenly a woman started to scream. The scream began, at first very deep, in the belly and became more and more shrill, deafening; it seemed to come from the top of the skull, you know, the fontanel, from which religions often say that the soul escapes at the moment of death. It's terrifying. That is poetry. I write between two doors, all of a sudden, like that woman who started to scream."[5] Her work became a kind of exorcism for the pain that came from the unbearable early loss of these two first loves. Years later, when asked why she did not have the violent character of her poetry, she answered: "If I did not write, perhaps I would embody my words. It's a kind of conjuration . . ."6

Mansour remained very private about her life and mostly refused to publish poems that were too directly autobiographical, such as the following one on her mother:

> Since yesterday you are dead my mother
> Deliver me from your suffering
> You are frozen with dread under your glass mask
> Deliver me from your maternal kisses
> That crawl on my kneeling body
> Like slugs
> For my eyes are stuck in the swamps of desire
> Deliver me from your heavy shadow
> My silted ovaries suffocate between your hands
> Deliver me from your absence
> Deliver me from the rain

Autobiographical elements in the poems she did publish were much more encrypted, with the crab often representing the cancer that had ended her mother's life:

> The crabs were fighting over your flesh
> Nothing remained of your chubby breasts.

In Mansour's work, love and death are inseparable. Rather than running from the dual traumas of her youth, she explored them, writing toward the demons that haunted her. A native English speaker, Mansour switched to writing in French when she met and married her second husband, Samir Mansour, a handsome and athletic Franco-Egyptian who was almost twice her age and of whom her family disapproved, due to his reputation as a womanizer. "I met a man who refused to speak anything other than French. So I dropped English and I started reading, writing, and trying to think in French. I started a new life with new thoughts. When I re-read the things I had written in English, it had nothing to do with anything, as though someone else had arrived at that moment."7 With a new husband, a new language, and a new life, Joyce Mansour tried to rid herself of the pain from the tragedies of her past. She never spoke of her first husband with Samir. The couple divided their life between Egypt and Europe, with properties in Cairo, Paris, and Alexandria, at the edge of the desert. "We crisscrossed the desert in a Jeep, looking for archeological sites. We slept outdoors. We divided the tasks."8 Through this newfound love, Mansour seemed to have escaped the worst of her despair.

The Mansours led a worldly life in Cairo, occasionally attending extravagant receptions hosted by Egypt's ruler, King Farouk. They also mixed with the diplomatic and business communities of the city. Joyce Mansour first encountered surrealism through a close friend of her husband, Marie Cavadia, who hosted the most important salon in Cairo and was a long-time patron of the Egyptian parasurrealist group Art and Liberty, founded in 1939 by Georges Henein, Ramses Younane, and Fouad Kamel.9 At Cavadia's salon, circa 1950, Mansour met Henein, who had recently broken with the French surrealist group, which was struggling to maintain its pre-war vigor. Over the years, Mansour would meet many significant artists and writers at the salon, including the novelist André Pieyre de Mandiargue and the science journalist Gérald Messadié, both of whom encouraged her to publish her work.10

In Paris, Mansour found her most decisive ally for publishing her work through the visual artist George Hugnet, a veteran of both Paris dada and surrealism who had just published his own book with Editions Seghers. She sent him a thick manuscript from which he helped her select the poems for her first book, *Cris (Screams)*. Many poems from the same manuscript would eventually be published in *Déchirures (Shreds)*. Hugnet sent the manuscript to Pierre Berger, an editor for the surrealist-friendly publisher Pierre Seghers. "The coincidence of a common friend allowed me to come across Joyce Mansour's manuscript," Berger recalled. "On the first page there were four letters: *Cris (Screams)*. From the very first poems, I understood their brutal meaning, and I saw the revolt hidden in their brevity. The screams of the poet hit me like surprising fist punches. They expressed the pathos of unusual days. . . I showed them to Pierre Seghers and Raymond Queneau. The enthusiasm I hoped for came from Pierre Seghers. *Screams* took its spot in the P.S. collection. As for Queneau, he never gave an answer."[11]

Screams appeared in December 1953, when Mansour, aged 25, was still living in Cairo. The collection of short poems was the most talked about publication in Egyptian literary circles, yet it was met with mixed reviews. Her friends indicated surprise, timidly acknowledging the originality of her voice, but expressing uneasiness about the content. They hoped that Mansour's somewhat bothersome poetic furor might be quieted. Mansour found herself isolated; "My father begged, 'Why don't you write about the bees and the flowers, instead of things like that?' and others would say, 'She's crazy. It's not even worth talking about.'"[12] "'Screaming' is not the best way to make yourself heard," wrote another critic. French poet Alain Bosquet wrote derisively in *Combat*: "Joyce Mansour, Egyptian and Lady of the high society, annexes necrophilia to poetry with extreme ease. The old boys will drool with joy. . . Don't give her access to the morgue: she'll wake the corpses."[13]

This last review, however, attracted André Breton's attention. In February of '54, Mansour sent him her book with a small dedication: "To Mr. André Breton, a few 'screams' as a tribute." André Breton responded, "I love, Madam, the scent of dark, ultra-dark, orchids in your poems." These are some of the first words of praise and encouragement that Mansour received for her work. The French surrealists immediately embraced her as one of their own. Jean-Louis Bédouin reviewed her work in the May issue of the surrealist review *Médium*: "There is nothing here that doesn't spill from the darkest depths of the soul, where love and death, distress and desire, pleasure and suffering fuse into a single all-consuming reality that consumes itself through the object of its own desire. . . It is essential in a time of pin-ups and cover-girls, in a time of learned ignorance about true human needs, that a woman reminds us that love is a tragic experience, vital, like hunger, and femininity is a force to be reckoned with, capable of violence and cruelty as well as tenderness and joy."[14] A few years later, in the group's official history of its activities after the Second World War, *Twenty Years of Surrealism: 1939–1959* (1961), Bédouin would identify *Cris* as "the poetic *event* of this year 1954. . . . From then on Joyce Mansour collaborated on all surrealist publications and brought to the life of the group a unique, irreplaceable element."[15]

While Mansour was still living in Cairo when her first book of poems was published, circumstances in Egypt would rapidly change, sending her and her entire family into permanent exile. In 1954, in the wake of the Egyptian Revolution of 1952 against King Farouk, and the establishment of the Republic of Egypt the following year, Gamal Abdel Nasser came to power. Shortly thereafter, his government seized most of her family's assets, including Mansour's childhood home, which now houses the Greek embassy in Cairo. Her father and brother were imprisoned by the government for several months and moved to Switzerland after their release. Joyce, her husband, and their young son Philippe (born in 1952) moved permanently to their home in Paris, never to set foot in Egypt again. In Paris, the family would expand with the birth of the Mansours' second son, Cyrille, in 1955.

Once settled in Paris, Mansour grew increasingly involved with the surrealists, becoming an intimate friend of André Breton, who became the greatest champion of her work. The two spent almost every afternoon together. She would visit him at his atelier at 42 rue Fontaine or they would go browsing flea markets, hunting for the uncanny objects of which they were both collectors. They grew so close that she was rumored to be his last great love.[16] While the two were never lovers, their friendship was one of mutual admiration, "fraternal and infinite" as she would describe it.[17] In an interview with *Le Monde* in 1962, Breton declared Mansour one of the three most important surrealist poets to emerge in the past 20 years, along with Jean-Pierre Duprey and Malcolm de Chazal. He never missed an opportunity to promote the work of this "female poet."

While Breton could be difficult to get along with, and frequently fell out with many in the surrealist movement, Mansour stayed out of such disputes. Indeed, she worked to mend many of the friendships Breton famously broke off, successfully orchestrating reconciliations, including several between Breton and Alain Jouffroy, a major postwar surrealist poet and theorist. Most significantly, Mansour oversaw the readmittance to Breton's group of the painter Roberto Matta, when she hosted at her Paris apartment the infamous 1959 performance piece *Exécution du testament du Marquis de Sade*, during which Canadian artist Jean Benoît branded himself with an iron spelling out SADE. Taking up Benoît's challenge—"Who's next?"—Matta "rushed up, tore open his shirt, and seared his own left breast," a dramatic gesture earning him reinstatement into the group.[18] Breton and Mansour remained intimate friends until his death in 1966. She dedicated several pieces to him, including the poetry collections *Carré blanc* (1966) and *Les Damnations* (1967).

Translation requires re-inhabiting the original process of creation. It asks for an intimate reading, as though one is slipping on a piece of clothing the author might have worn. Mansour's poetry is both a challenge and a pleasure to translate. Her words are heavy with emotion as she tests us with constant provocations and inversions of traditional narratives and beliefs. Our accepted logic dictates that what is dead rots, but she uses phrases like "all that is alive rots";[19] in another poem ("Worn Shadow") she describes life as "painful for the dead." In "Flowered Like Lewdness," the objectifying gaze of an unidentified man clashes with Mansour's morbid version of the feminine. For him women are "canons of delirium," to which the speaker replies that she only "savor(s) death." In "Nursery Rhyme for a Courtesan," magnolias, normally a symbol of beauty, femininity, and purity, become "cannibalistic." Beauty is repulsive, orgasm is death, death is life, and fantasies, like women, become all too real.

Mansour took some of her inspiration from ancient religions and traditions, including Ancient Egypt, where death is not considered to be the end of life, but rather a transition to another reality. A great deal of Mansour's work centers around female figures in religion, such as Mary,

Lilith, or Miriam; indeed, Jean-Louis Bédouin intuited this connection as early as his first appreciation of *Cris* in *Médium*, writing that her poems "evoke the savage grandeur of the rare hymns to Selene known to us, magical invocations addressed to the 'fawn killer' of bloody nocturnal divinity by the Bacchantes, the enemies of Orpheus."[20] Several of her poems, including the untitled one below, evoke the Egyptian goddess of the sky, Nut, whose naked body was covered with stars and was arched protectively over her husband, Geb, the earth god. Nut swallowed the sun god Ra in the evening and gave birth to him each morning.[21]

> A woman created the sun
> Inside her
> And her hands were beautiful
> The earth plunged beneath her feet
> Assailing her with the fertile breath
> Of volcanoes
> Her nostrils quivered her eyelids drooped
> Weighed down by the heavy silt of the pillow
> It is night
> And the calm wound where the breathless void dies
> Strikes, struggles, opens and quietly closes
> on the swaying rod of Noah the explorer[22]

It's not difficult to see how a narrative with a goddess—rather than a god—of the cosmos inspired Mansour to imagine a richer and more complex story about life, death, and gender than what was on offer in her adoptive country of France. While her writing has strong feminist leanings, she remained independent of the movement: "I don't know what you're talking about," she once responded when asked to contribute to a feminist magazine.[23] Although she was taken seriously by the surrealists, who were mildly more progressive toward women than previous French literary movements, beyond that she received limited recognition. Even the surrealist movement, which embraced her work, was known to insist on the role of women as muse or *femme-enfant*, the child-woman.[24] Meret Oppenheim, a surrealist artist who eventually distanced herself from the movement, famously said, "The (Surrealist) women were loved, but only as women."[25] Mansour remained a lifelong surrealist, even as she maintained a certain independence from any doctrinaire form of surrealism. Her work clearly defies the confines placed on women by evoking both the creative and destructive sides of female power.[26] Her version of femininity is authentic and complicated. It mixes irony, rage, and vulnerability while mocking the superficial ideal of women as innocent, submissive, or delicate objects of desire. In the poem "Dowsing," Mansour uses her signature dark sense of humor to satirize articles like "The Good House Wife's Guide" published by *Housekeeping Monthly*, unleashing her anger in her advice to women experiencing the sting of neglect or betrayal in their marriage. "Husband neglecting you?" she asks. "Invite his mother to sleep in your room / ... / piss in his soup when he lies down happily next to you[.]"

Among the earliest selections from the poems in this volume, I translated two poems from her 1965 collection *Carré blanc*. The title literally translates as *White Square* and refers to the symbol that appeared on French television to alert viewers of adult content. Mansour wrote the poems during a prolonged separation from her husband, after she had grown tired of Sam's frequent infidelities; his betrayals caused her to re-experience the traumatic losses of her youth.[27] The poems' speaker moves among rage, desire, and sadness, unashamed of her frustrations and solitude. Throughout this collection she is angry and defiant: In "Woman Warrior in Love," she promises to devour "he who would broadside me" and advises that "one must learn to wait to take revenge." In "Sun in Capricorn" the speaker struggles with her longing in the face of an impassive interlocutor: "I can't breathe without your mouth" and "Your hand thunders indifference." As Alain Jouffroy said of her writing, Mansour delivers "indiscrete truths" and her absence of modesty "is a kind of feminine rebellion against the sexual despotism of man who often makes eroticism his own exclusive creation."[28]

After Breton's death, Mansour remained active within the surrealist group until Breton's successor, Jean Schuster, decided to dissolve the group in 1969 after the events of the 1968 general strike. The group felt that the movement had become sufficiently widespread in the youth culture that the meetings were no longer necessary. Furthermore, an increasing number of students had started to attend the regular café meetings, making them untenable. Not all the members of the group agreed with the dissolution; some of them continued holding meetings after the group's dissolution, and Mansour would participate in various successor groups. Beyond that, Mansour continued to nurture close and intimate friendships and collaborations with surrealist visual artists, including Pierre Alechinsky, Enrico Baj, Jorge Camacho, Wilfredo Lam, Roberto Matta, and Pierre Molinier. Always in urgent need of intimate friendships, she also grew close with Henri Michaux (himself never a member of Breton's group) during her separations with her husband.[29] She continued writing poetry until her death from cancer, in 1986, at the age of 58.

Mansour was known and respected within surrealist circles as André Breton championed her work, but beyond those, she was ignored. Her use of irony mixed with the erotic macabre shows similarities with the work of much more renowned French poets: She is a Baudelaire minus the shame or a Georges Bataille *au feminin*. And yet her books, once published by surrealist presses, are largely out of print in France. A collection of her complete works in French—which includes both short fiction and poetry collections—was published in 2014 by Michel de Maule but is increasingly difficult to find. That same year, her daughter-in-law published her biography, but it too is becoming rare, as has the earlier, pioneering biography, *Joyce Mansour: Une étrange demoiselle* (2005) by Marie-Laure Missir. Over the years, there have been English translations of selections of her work, but most are also out of print.[30]

Giving Joyce Mansour her rightful place in literature is no easy task. She was an immigrant in post-war France and her favorite subject matter happened to be two of society's greatest fears: death and unfettered female desire. "Even in death I will return to this world to fornicate" is an often-quoted statement from Mansour's short story collection, *Les Gisants Satisfaits (The Satisfied Statues)*.[31] If writing for her was a conjuration of her

11

own demons, then surely translating her words can serve to summon a spirit so keen to return from the world of the dead. There is no better time than now for Mansour to make a comeback and be given the space and recognition that her work rightly deserves.

ENDNOTES

1. J. H. Matthews, "The Poetry of Joyce Mansour," *Books Abroad* 40, no. 3 (1966): 284–85. https://doi.org/10.2307/40120803.

2. Marie-Francine Desvaux-Mansour, "Le Surréalisme à travers Joyce Mansour Tome 1" (Ph.D. diss., Université de Paris 1 Panthéon-Sorbonne, 2014), 25. https://ecm.univ-paris1.fr/nuxeo/site/.../6832d455-5fd3-4ae3-ad61-1dd4384ae368. Accessed July 14, 2018.

3. Marie-Laure Missir, *Joyce Mansour: Une étrange demoiselle* (Paris: Jean-Michel Place, 2005), 20.

4. Missir, *Joyce Mansour: Une étrange demoiselle*, 20.

5. Missir, *Joyce Mansour: Une étrange demoiselle*, 28.

6. Desvaux-Mansour, "Le Surréalisme à travers Joyce Mansour Tome 1," 385.

7. Missir, *Joyce Mansour: Une étrange demoiselle*, 21.

8. Missir, *Joyce Mansour: Une étrange demoiselle*, 28.

9. Missir, *Joyce Mansour: Une étrange demoiselle*, 22, dates the group from 1938 but Samir Gharieb, in his *Surrealism in Egypt and Plastic Arts* (Guizeh, Egypt: Prism Publications, 1986), 1, gives the oddly specific date of January 9, 1939.

10. See generally Missir, *Joyce Mansour: Une étrange demoiselle*, 22–24.

11. Missir, *Joyce Mansour: Une étrange demoiselle*, 26–27.

12. Missir, *Joyce Mansour: Une étrange demoiselle*, 30.

13. Missir, *Joyce Mansour: Une étrange demoiselle*, 30.

14. Missir, *Joyce Mansour: Une étrange demoiselle*, 31. For the original, half-column review, see Jean-Louis Bédouin, "Joyce Mansour," *Médium: Communication surréaliste*, New Series, No. 3 (May 1954), 42.

15. Jean-Louis Bédouin, *Vingt ans de surréalisme: 1939–1959* (Paris: Denoël, 1961), 269.

16. Missir, *Joyce Mansour: Une étrange demoiselle*, 54. The desire to subsume Mansour's poetic achievements into her relationship with André Breton persists to this day. In 2020, one of her French publishers said to me outright, "You know something, I never met Joyce Mansour but I have a friend who did and he told me that without André Breton there would BE NO Joyce Mansour."

Perhaps nothing underlines the need for this book more clearly.

17. Missir, *Joyce Mansour: Une étrange demoiselle*, 54.

18. See Mark Polizzotti, *Revolution of the Mind: The Life of André Breton* (London: Bloomsbury, 1995), 605–606, for an account of this evening.

19. Joyce Mansour, *Carré Blanc* (1965), in *Œuvres complètes Joyce Mansour: Prose et poésie* (Paris: Michel de Maule, 2014), 406.

20. Bédouin, "Joyce Mansour," 42.

21. S. T. Hollis, "Women of Ancient Egypt and the Sky Goddess Nut," *The Journal of American Folklore* 100, No. 398 (1987): 496–503.

22. Joyce Mansour, *Rapaces* (Paris: Seghers, 1960), 78.

23. Marie-Francine Desvaux-Mansour, *Une vie surréaliste: Joyce Mansour, complice d'André Breton* (Paris: France-Empire, 2014), 111.

24. J. Preckshot, "Identity Crises in Joyce Mansour Narratives," in *Surrealism and Women*, eds. Mary Ann Caws, Rudolf Kenzli, and Raaberg Raaberg (Cambridge, MA: MIT Press, 1991), 98.

25. Marylaura Papalas, "Female Violence as Social Power: Joyce Mansour's Surrealist Anti-Muse," in *Rebelles et criminelles chez les écrivaines d'expression française*, eds. F. Chevillot and C. Trout (Amsterdam: Editions Rodopi B.V., 2013), 204.

26. M. De Julia, "Joyce Mansour and Egyptian Mythology," in *Surrealism and Women*, eds. Mary Ann Caws, Rudolf Kenzli, and Raaberg Raaberg (Cambridge, MA: MIT Press, 1991), 117.

27. Desvaux-Mansour, "Le Surréalisme à travers Joyce Mansour Tome 1," 488.

28. "Joyce Mansour *Oeuvres Complètes*," https://www.micheldemaule.com/fr/livres-parus/Jouce-Mansour-Oeuvres-completes/375.htm. Accessed on July 14, 2018.

29. See Mary Ann Caws, "Joyce Mansour in Double Time," in *Symbolism, Dada, Surréalism: Selected Essays* (London and Chicago: Reaction Books, forthcoming).

30. The exception is the bilingual selection *Essential Poems and Writings by Joyce Mansour*, trans. Serge Gavronsky (Boston, MA: Black Widow Press, 2008).

31. Joyce Mansour, "Marie ou l'Honneur de Servir," in *Œuvres complètes Joyce Mansour: Prose et poésie* (Paris: Michel de Maule, 2014), 46.

Editorial Note

Garrett Caples

Many of the original publications of Joyce Mansour's poetry are so rare as to be unobtainable. Worldcat.org, for example, lists exactly one copy of her *Jasmine d'hiver* (1982)—at the Bibliothèque Nationale! Our sources for most of our texts in the original French therefore are the two posthumous collections of her work: *Prose & poésie: œuvre complète* (Arles, France: Actes Sud, 1991) and *Œuvres complètes: prose & poésie* (Paris: Michel de Maule, 2014). (All indications suggest that the latter volume is simply a scan of the former.) Two poems from Mansour's debut *Cris*—"Fièvre ton sexe est un crabe" and "Une femme créait le soliel"—are drawn from earlier published versions; our source is the text of *Cris* reproduced in Mansour's third book, *Rapaces* (Paris: Seghers, 1960), pages 77 and 78.

We also fortunately had access to a collection of the complete run of *Bief: jonction surréaliste* (Paris: Le Terrain Vague, 1958–1960), against which we were able to compare the versions in the two collected editions. These poems appear in the order in which they published, with the exception of the last three poems listed—"Ce qui se porte cet hiver," "Ce qui ne se porte pas cet hiver," and "Conseils d'une consœur"—which are in fact the earliest of the group (*Bief* No. 1, November 15, 1958). The reason for this relocation is that, like the sequence "Le Missel de la Miss (Bonnes nuits)," these poems plus the opening selection from *Rapaces*, "Rhabdomancie," were grouped together in *Bief* under the general title "Prête, à portée" (itself a play on the French phrase for "ready to wear," prête-à-porter, which might translate as "ready, and easy"). Given that she collected it in *Rapaces* without including the rest of the sequence, she clearly valued "Rhabdomancie" above the other three, so we didn't feel we should subsume it into "Prête, à portée." But by relocating the first three sections of "Prête, à portée" to the end of the selections from *Bief*, we provide the opportunity to read that sequence intact, while nonetheless according "Rhabdomancie" its proper location as an individual poem from *Rapaces*.

Otherwise, while not drawing on every poetry book she published, *Emerald Wounds* nonetheless attempts to give a sense of her career arc as a poet. Past translations of Mansour have tended to emphasize her earlier work—from *Cris* in 1954 through the dissolution of the surrealist group in 1969—at the expense of her later volumes. Given that there is so little Mansour presently available in English, we couldn't neglect her writing of the '50s and '60s, but we have attempted to balance this with full-book presentations of *Pandémonium* (1976), *Jasmin d'hiver* (1982), and *Trous noirs* (1986), along with some selections from *Flammes immobiles* (1985).

There's a paucity of biographical information on Joyce Mansour in English, and we wish to acknowledge our reliance on the two major French sources on her life: *Joyce Mansour: Une étrange demoiselle* (2005) by Marie-Laure Missir and *Une vie surréaliste: Joyce Mansour, complice d'André Breton* (2014) by Marie-Francine Mansour.

We would also like to thank the following for various forms of assistance in the making of this book: Olivier Brossard, Mary Ann Caws, Norma Cole, Emma Hager, Andrew Joron, Elaine Katzenberger, Catherine Moorhouse, Owen Moorhouse, Nancy J. Peters, and Kit Schluter. Finally, we are grateful to Cyrille Mansour and the Estate of Joyce Mansour for making this volume possible.

EMERALD WOUNDS

Je te soulève dans mes bras
Pour la dernière fois.
Je te dépose hâtivement dans ton cercueil bon marché.
Quatre hommes l'épaulent après l'avoir cloué
Sur ton visage défait sur tes membres angoissés.
Ils descendent en jurant les escaliers étroits
Et toi tu bouges dans ton monde étriqué.
Ta tête détachée de ta gorge coupée
C'est le commencement de l'éternité.

I lift you in my arms
For the last time.
I hastily place you into your cheap coffin.
Four men lift it once they've nailed the lid
On your undone face on your anguished limbs.
They go down the narrow stairs swearing
And you are moving in your narrow world.
Your head removed from your slit throat
It is the beginning of eternity.

L'amazone mangeait son dernier sein.
La nuit avant la bataille finale
Son cheval chauve respirait l'air frais de la mer
En piaffant en rageant en hennissant sa peur
Car les dieux descendaient des monts de la science
Apportant avec eux les hommes
et les tanks.

The amazon was eating her last breast.
The night before the final battle
Her shaved horse breathed the fresh air of the ocean
Stomping, gnawing, whining with fear
For the gods were descending from the mounts of science
Bringing with them the men
and the tanks.

Chien bleu nez enfoncé dans la terre
La tête foisonnante de cris de chasse d'amour
D'amour gaspillé.
Les feuillages de la forêt le connaissent
Ils le chassent de leurs mains rousses.
Chien bleu animal sans secours
Nourris-toi du sang des pauvres
Pour être aimé il faut être cruel.
Animal si tu veux être domestique
Vends ton âme aux hommes.

Blue dog whose nose is buried in the sand
Head filled with cries of the hunt for love
Of wasted love.
The foliages of the forest are used to it
They hunt it with their red hands.
Blue dog unrescued animal
Feed yourself with the blood of the poor
To be loved one must be cruel.
Animal, if you wish to be domesticated
Sell your soul to men.

Je veux me montrer nue à tes yeux chantants.
Je veux que tu me voies criant de plaisir.
Que mes membres pliés sous un poids trop lourd
Te poussent à des actes impies.
Que les cheveux lisses de ma tête offerte
S'accrochent à tes ongles courbés de fureur.
Que tu te tiennes debout aveugle et croyant
Regardant le haut de mon corps déplumé.

I want to be naked in your singing eyes.
I want you to see me crying out from pleasure.
That my limbs folded under a weight too heavy
Push you to impious acts.
That the silky hair on my offered head
Clings to your furiously bent fingernails.
That you stand up, blind and believing
Looking at the top of my plucked body.

Ton cou est un mât où pend ta tête
Flottant dans le vide ton corps me supplie
Me supplie de souffler dans ta bouche ouverte
Les mots veules
De mon désir.

Ton enfant dans tes bras.
Sa tête profile contre le noir de ta poitrine
Ses yeux sans vision ses mains sans proie.
Ton corps me prie
De donner en gage
Ma vie.

Your neck is a pole where your head hangs
Floating in the void your body begs me
Begs me to blow into your open mouth
The empty words
Of my desire.

Your child in your arms
His head profiled against the black of your chest
His sightless eyes his empty hands
Your body prays for me
To give as a pledge
My life.

Fièvre ton sexe est un crabe
Fièvre les chats se nourrissent à tes mamelles vertes
Fièvre la hâte de tes mouvements de reins
L'avidité de tes muqueuses cannibales
L'étreinte de tes tubes qui tressaillent et qui clament
Déchirent mes doigts de cuir
Arrachent mes pistons
Fièvre éponge mort gonflée de mollesse
Ma bouche court le long de ta ligne d'horizon
Voyageuse sans peur sur une mer de frénésie

Fever your sex is a crab
Fever the cats feed on your green nipples
Fever the quick movement of your lower back
The eagerness of your cannibalistic tissues
The grip of your tubes that quiver and cry out
Tear my leather fingers
Snatch at my pistons
Fever dead sponge bloated with softness
My mouth runs along your horizon
A traveler unafraid on a frenzied sea

Une femme créait le soleil
En elle
Et ses mains étaient belles
La terre plongeait sous ses pieds
L'assaillant de l'haleine fertile
Des volcans
Ses narines palpitaient ses paupières se baissaient
Empesées par le lourd limon de l'oreiller
C'est la nuit
Et l'égratignure tranquille où meurt le vide haletant
Se bat se débat s'ouvre et doucement se ferme
Sur la verge dodelinante de Noé l'explorateur

A woman created the sun
Inside her
And her hands were beautiful
The earth plunged beneath her feet
Assailing her with the fertile breath
Of volcanoes
Her nostrils quivered her eyelids drooped
Weighed down by the heavy silt of the pillow
It is night
And the calm wound where the breathless void dies
Strikes, struggles, opens and quietly closes
on the swaying rod of Noah the explorer

Couchée sur mon lit
Je vois ton visage reflété sur le mur
Ton corps sans ombre qui fait peur au mien
Tes allées et venues frénétiques et cadencées
Tes grimaces qui font fuir tous les meubles de la pièce
Sauf le lit ancré par ma sueur de mensonges
Et moi qui attends sans couverture ni espoir
L'angoisse.

Lying on my bed
I see your face reflected on the wall
Your shadowless body that frightens mine
Your clocked and frenetic coming and going
Your scowl from which every piece of furniture flees
Except for the bed anchored by my sweat of lies
And me who waits with neither blankets nor hope
for angst.

J'ai un esprit inquiet.
Il habite près du lac que sont mes yeux enfoncés.
Il s'agite sous le soleil ardent de mes prières
Il dort et ses rêves frissonnent sous ma peau
Créant l'angoisse dans mon cœur chantant.

I have a worried mind.
It lives next to the lake that are my sunken eyes.
It moves under the glowing sun of my prayers
It sleeps and its dreams shiver under my skin
Creating fear in my singing heart.

Combien d'amours ont fait crier ton lit?
Combien d'années ont ridé tes yeux?
Qui a vidé tes seins épuisés?
Je t'ai regardé avec mes yeux de plomb
Et mes illusions ont éclaté
Laissant derrière elles
Ta vieillesse
Qui ne peux répondre à mes questions.

How many loves made your bed cry out?
How many years have wrinkled your eyes?
Who emptied your drained breasts?
I watched you with my crushing eyes
And my illusions burst
Leaving behind them
Your old age
That cannot answer my questions.

Coquillage qui traîne sur une plage déserte
Caressé d'un doigt distrait par la mer
Qui laisse derrière elle sa trace baveuse
Qui attire malgré elle l'ennemi.
Il approche il l'immobilise d'une main fouineuse
Il lui sort son âme de son lit douillet
Et aspire son agonie.

Seashell lying on an empty beach
Touched by a distracted finger of the sea
Leaving a frothy trail behind her
Luring the enemy despite herself.
He approaches and pins her with a prying hand
He removes her soul from the comfort of her bed
And sucks on her agony.

Que mes seins te provoquent
Je veux ta rage.
Je veux voir tes yeux s'épaissir
Tes joues blanchir en se creusant.
Je veux tes frissons.
Je veux que tu éclates entre mes cuisses
Que mes désirs soient exaucés sur le sol fertile
De ton corps sans pudeur.

May my breasts provoke you
I want your rage.
I want to see your eyes thicken
Your cheeks turn white as they sink.
I want your shudders.
I want you to burst between my thighs
That my desires be satiated on the fertile soil
Of your shameless body.

Invitez-moi à passer la nuit dans votre bouche
Racontez-moi la jeunesse des rivières
Pressez ma langue contre votre œil de verre
Donnez-moi votre jambe comme nourrice
Et puis dormons, frère de mon frère,
Car nos baisers meurent plus vite que la nuit.

Invite me to spend the night in your mouth
Tell me about the youth of rivers
Press my tongue against your glass eye
Give me your leg as a wet nurse
And let's sleep, brother of my brother,
For our kisses die faster than the night.

II n'y a pas de mots
Seulement des poils
Dans le monde sans verdure
Où mes seins sont rois.
Il n'y a pas de gestes
Seulement ma peau
Et les fourmis qui grouillent entre mes jambes onctueuses
Portent des masques du silence en travaillant.
Viens la nuit et ton extase
Et mon corps profond de ce poulpe sans pensée
Avale ton sexe agité
Pendant sa naissance.

There are no words
Only hairs
In a world without greenery
Where my breasts are kings.
There are no deeds
Only my skin
And the ants that crawl between my unctuous legs
Carry masks of silence while laboring.
Come night and your bliss
And my deep body, mindless octopus
Swallows your excited cock
As it is born.

Hurlements d'une montagne qui accouche
La mer sa sœur arrête ses fols amours
La campagne dénudée arrête sa course éperdue
Et renvoie le vent son amant.
Car le veau d'or apparaîtra des flancs en labeur
Il arrivera sans tache des entrailles contractée
Prêt à être Dieu pour nous, gens de peu d'amour,
Moïse préparez-vous.

Shrieks from a mountain giving birth
Her sister the ocean ceases her wild mating
The naked countryside ceases her frantic chase
And rebuffs her lover the wind.
For the golden calf will appear from the laboring flanks
He will arrive unstained from the contracting entrails
Ready to be God for us, people of so little love,
Moses prepare yourself.

Je suis la nuit

Cette nuit d'espace glacée par la froide imbécilité de la lune.

Je suis l'argent

L'argent qui fait l'argent sans savoir pourquoi.

Je suis l'homme

L'homme qui presse la gâchette et tire l'émotion

Pour mieux vivre.

I am the night
This night of space frozen by the cold idiocy of the moon.
I am money
Money that makes money without knowing why.
I am man
Man who pulls the trigger and shoots emotion
To live better.

C'était hier.
Le premier poète urinait son amour
Son sexe en deuil chantait bruyamment
Les chansons gutturales
Des montagnes
Le premier dieu debout sur son halo
Annonçait sa venue sur la terre évanouie
C'était demain.
Mais les hommes à tête-de-chat
Mangeaient leurs yeux brouillés
Sans remarquer leurs églises qui brûlaient
Sans sauver leur âme qui fuyait
Sans saluer leurs dieux qui mouraient
C'était la guerre.

It was yesterday.
The first poet pissed his love
His cock in mourning sang loudly
Guttural songs
From the mountains
The first god standing on his halo
Announced his arrival on a passed-out earth
It was tomorrow.
But men with cat-heads
Were eating their scrambled eyes
Without noticing their burning churches
Without saving their fleeing souls
Without greeting their dying gods
It was war.

La nappe rouge
Tachée de sang
Pend sur les épaules de la statue de bronze.
Les souris du désir
Mangent le sexe cru
Caché dans la main
Du sculpteur
Fou.

The red tablecloth
Stained with blood
Hangs from the shoulders of the bronze statue.
The mice of desire
Eat the raw cock
Hidden in the hand
Of the sculptor
Gone mad.

Pleure petit homme
Ton bateau est à vendre
Ta femme vendue
Et le lait frais de ta vache
Rouge du sang des nègres
Fait pisser tes enfants
De haine.

Cry little man
Your boat is for sale
Your wife is sold
And the fresh milk of your cow
Red with the blood of blacks
Makes your children piss
Their hate.

La mort est une marguerite qui dort
Aux pieds d'une madone en chaleur
Et les mille délicates puanteurs
Sombres comme une aisselle, saignantes comme un cœur
Dorment elles aussi dans les corps des femmes nues
Qui couchent dans les champs ou qui cherchent dans les rues
La fraise mal dorée de l'amour.

Death is a daisy sleeping
At the foot of a madonna in heat
And those thousand delicate odors
Dark like an armpit, bloody like a heart
Also sleep in the bodies of naked women
Who bed in the fields or search the streets
For the poorly gilded strawberry of love.

Danse avec moi, petit violoncelle
Sur l'herbe mauve magique
Des nuits de pleine lune.
Danse avec moi, petite note de musique
Parmi les œufs durs, les violons, les clystères.
Chante avec moi, petite sorcière
Car les pierres tournent en rond
Autour des soupières
Où se noie la musique
Des réverbères.

Dance with me, little cello
On the magic purple grass
During nights of the full moon.
Dance with me, little music note
Among the hard-boiled eggs, the violins, the enemas.
Sing with me, little witch
For the stones go in circles
Around the soup bowls
Where drowns the music
Of streetlights.

La marée monte sous la pleine lune des aveugles.
Seule avec les coquillage et l'eau glauque du petit jour
Solitaire sur la plage mon lit lentement se noie.
La marée monte dans le ciel titubant d'amour
Sans dents dans la forêt j'attends ma mort, muette,
Et la marée monte dans ma gorge où meurt un papillon.

The tide is rising under the full moon of the blind.
Alone with the seashells and the murky water of daybreak
Alone on the beach my bed is slowly drowning.
The tide is rising in the sky reeling with love
Toothless in the forest I wait for my death, silent,
And the tide is rising in my throat where a butterfly dies.

J'ai volé l'oiseau jaune
Qui vit dans le sexe du diable
Il m'apprendra comment séduire
Les hommes, les cerfs, les anges aux ailes doubles,
Il ôtera ma soif, mes vêtements, mes illusions,
Il dormira,
Mais moi, mon sommeil court sur les toits
Murmurant, gesticulant, faisant l'amour violemment,
Avec des chats.

I stole the yellow bird
That lives in the devil's sex
He will teach me how to seduce
Men, stags, double-winged angels,
He will remove my thirst, my clothes, my illusions,
He will sleep,
As for me, my slumber runs along the rooftops
Mumbling, waving, making violent love,
With cats.

Je veux dormir avec toi coude à coude
Cheveux entremêlés
Sexes noués
Avec ta bouche comme oreiller.
Je veux dormir avec toi dos à dos
Sans haleine pour nous séparer
Sans mots pour nous distraire
Sans yeux pour nous mentir
Sans vêtements.
Je veux dormir avec toi sein contre sein
Crispée en sueur
Brillant de mille frissons
Mangée par l'inertie folle de l'extase
Écartelée sur ton ombre
Martelée par ta langue
Pour mourir entre les dents cariées de lapin
Heureuse.

I want to sleep with you elbow to elbow
Hair entwined
Genitals enlaced
With your mouth as a pillow.
I want to sleep with you back to back
Without breath to keep us apart
Without words to distract us
Without eyes to tell lies
Without clothes.
I want to sleep with you breast to breast
Clenched and sweating
Glistening from a thousand shivers
Consumed by the wild inertia of bliss
Splayed on your shadow
Pounded by your tongue
And to die between the rotted teeth of a rabbit
Contented.

L'orage tire une marge argentée
Dans le ciel
Et éclate dans un immense spasme englué
Sur la terre.
L'écume flottante
Envolée de la mer en déroute
Vient rafraîchir nos visages défaits
Et nos corps qui se cachent
Dans la sombre tiédeur de nos désirs endormis
Se dressent.
Notre sieste harcelée de punaises
Prend fin
Et le court lapement des vagues
Sur la plage où danse l'azur
S'est tu, mon amour
Et il pleut.

The storm draws a silver line
In the sky
And bursts into a great viscous spasm
On the earth.
The floating foam
Surge of the ocean in disarray
Refreshes our undone faces
And our bodies hiding
In the dark warmth of our sleeping desires
Rear themselves.
Our nap hassled by sleep bugs
Ends
And the short lapping of the waves
On the beach where the sky dances
Is quiet, my love
And it's raining.

LE MISSEL DE LA MISS (BONNES NUITS)

I. QUELQUES CONSEILS EN COURANT SUR QUATRE ROUES

Votre mari méprise vos tentatives d'accrochage?
N'hésitez pas à changer de vitesse au milieu de la nuit.
Surveillez ses cadrans : huile, température d'eau, essence.
S'il martyrise vos pneus
Embrayez à fond et utilisez au maximum votre petit frein moteur
N'accélérez jamais quand s'allume son clignoteur
Consultez plutôt votre témoin le rétroviseur
Et rangez-vous à droite sans trop vous trémousser.
Au premier indice de manœuvre amorcée
Dévoilez avec avarice vos bourrelets protecteurs
On ne peut être assez sûr du bon fonctionnement de ses phares.

THE MISSAL OF THE MISSUS (GOOD NIGHTS)

I. ADVICE FOR RUNNING ON FOUR WHEELS

Does your husband despise your collision attempts?
Don't hesitate to change gears in the middle of the night.
Check his gauges: oil, water temperature, gas.
If he torments your tires
Engage the clutch and maximize your little engine break
Never accelerate when the turn signal goes on
Instead turn to your witness the rearview mirror
And move to the right lane without too much shaking.
At the first hint of a maneuver
Reveal with greed your protective love handles
One can never be too sure of the efficiency of headlights.

II. IL FAIT FROID? UNE ROBE S'IMPOSE

Prenez deux torchons en peau d'amant maure
Tordez vos mains en leur donnant de l'éclat et des mancherons
Viendront embellir vos bras raccourcis par la lessive
Agrafez une martingale-pêcheuse sur votre plissé soleil
Coupez en biais (il ne faut pas que la queue dépasse)
Nouez la poitrine

Laissez tomber les pans
Jusqu'à l'ourlet
Devant.
Posé sur votre plage
Un noeud chapelier fera merveille
Des gants blancs un style jeune
Et le tour est joué (il est de taille)

II. COLD OUT? A DRESS IS ESSENTIAL

Take two tea towels of moorish lover's skin
Twist your hands giving them shine, and cap sleeves
Will beautify your arms shrunk in the wash
Staple a purple-martingale on your pleated sun
Cut on the bias (the tail must not protrude)
Tie the chest

Let the sides fall
Down to the hem
In front.
Placed on your beach
A hatters knot will do wonders
White gloves young style
And the trap is set (in plus size)

III. LIGNES AUTOUR D'UN CERCLE

La mode du haut de son sautoir
Dicte ordonne trépigne:
Creusez le ventre haussez le ton
Je ne veux ni fil ni pile
Ni bahut ni car
Gondolez les motifs
Voyez net et de loin
Corrigez la silhouette sans comprimer les organes
Je veux des formes avantageuses
Des bustes réglables à volonté
Des frissons combustibles éclairs
Fourrez la baleine dans le secret des panneaux
Tâchez la mousse de fleurettes à carreaux
Gonflez gonflez l'emballage doit être tubulaire
Et même une boulangère doit savoir plaire.

III. LINES AROUND A CIRCLE

Fashion from the heights of her necklace
Dictates, commands and chomps at the bit:
Dig out the belly raise your voice
I want neither thread nor pile
Neither sideboard nor bus
Warp the patterns
Clear and far sighted
Straighten the silhouette without crushing the organs
I want ample shapes
Busts with unlimited alterations
Shudders flammable flashes
Stuff the whale in the secret of the panels
Stain the tiled whipping foam
Blow blow the wrapping must be tubular
Even the baker woman must know how to please.

GENÈVE

De mon lit j'imagine l'étrange quiétude du cimetière. Je me trémousse à l'idée du sang répandu; mes joues brûlent, mes dents immondes croquent le harpon glissant de la démence et je râle dans le noir comme une langouste aplatie.

Une touffe de tes cheveux titube sur la tombe. Ma poitrine se gerce de mille vaguelettes, agitées; je crois entendre les cris de nos parents, ces ténias sans opacité même dans la douleur—qui sillonnent les allées aux murs maussades de mousse, ils crient et se lamentent, propageant ainsi mon plaisir aux spasmes coulissants jusqu'au fin fond du jardin. Beau jardin aux silences de pommes de pin, aux rêves de marbre et de poulpes, aux sortilèges de blatte et aux douces odeurs de femme. J'écraserai mon cigare dans ton œil poché de veilles, j'écraserai ton pénis de mon talon éculé, je t'écraserai tout entier dans la puanteur de mon refus.

Ta voix perce la cloison. Tu te plains. Mon vagin se resserre. S'attendrir, et puis attendre...

GENEVA

From my bed I imagine the strange quiet of the graveyard. I fidget at the thought of spilled blood; my cheeks burn, my foul teeth bite the slippery harpoon of dementia and I moan in the dark like a flattened crayfish.

A tuft of your hair lurches on my tomb. My chest is chapped by a thousand wavelets, restless; I think I hear the screams of our parents, those tapeworms without opacity even in pain—who criss cross the alleys with sullen mossy walls, they scream and lament, spreading my spasmic delight all the way to the back of the garden. Beautiful garden with pinecone silences, with marble and octopus dreams, with cockroach spells and soft womanly smells. I will crush my cigar in your eye poached by late nights, I will crush your penis with my tired heel, I will crush you completely in the stench of my refusal.

Your voice breaks the divide. You're complaining. My vagina tightens. To be touched, and then to wait...

CONSEILS PRATIQUES EN ATTENDANT

La peinture constamment renouvelée du visage, les soins d'un corps toujours prêt, les courses à l'habillement, tout ceci vous confère votre dignité de femme mais, pour être femme, il ne suffit pas d'être belle, il faut aussi savoir attendre.

Savoir attendre sous une ombrelle, inquiète, jalouse, nonchalante de fatigue, l'arrivée du vieux Turc, messager d'un autre monde, le coup d'épée d'un crédule ou les moqueries d'un passant. Esclave des circonstances, attendre sans vanité, sans calcul et libre, le caprice du bazar; attendre sans plaisir la routine ou la chance.

Sachez attendre tout en restant jolie, détendue, nette... malgré la fuite des heures plus élastique que votre gaine (portez-la à toute heure: elle empêche l'angoisse de s'imposer entre les côtes et le grand sympathique, accélérant ainsi la disparition de votre vrai visage). Il faut savoir tromper son ennui. Attendre sans en avoir l'air et gare aux vieillissements! L'attente usera d'autant plus vos nerfs si la toile laisse passer les rayons du couchant.

Attendez dans une gare si l'étranger vous attire, mais apprenez à prévoir et détecter les pannes; devenez une conductrice expérimentée, une habile tricoteuse, une technicienne de l'aiguillage (tout ceci en six séances grâce à la nouvelle section pratique "Initiation à la loco-émotivité") avant de croiser le fer avec la chance. Couchez-vous ailleurs que sur les rails si vos bas ne sont pas de la meilleure qualité; tout le monde connaît la force du mimétisme (la statistique le prouve: de beaux traits font naître des points d'exclamation, des ronds-de-cuir, des tomates, etc.). Malgré cela ne vous couchez pas sur les rails; le train s'arrêtera sans votre participation, il a l'habitude, vous non.

PRACTICAL ADVICE WHILE YOU WAIT

Regularly applied makeup, thorough body care, shopping for outfits, all of these confer your dignity as a woman, but, to be a woman, beauty is not enough, one must also know how to wait.

Know how to wait under a parasol, worried, jealous, nonchalant from exhaustion, the arrival of an old Turk, messenger from another world, a sword strike of the gullible or the mocking of a passer-by. Slave of circumstances, to wait with no pride, free without a plan, the whim of a bazaar ; to wait without pleasure, for routine or for luck.

Know how to wait while staying pretty, relaxed, sharp . . . despite the whittling away of hours more elastic than your girdle (wear it at all hours: it prevents anxiety from building between the ribs and the sympathetic nerve, accelerating the disappearance of your real face). One must know how to fool your ennui. To wait without seeming to and watch out for aging! The wait will wear down your nerves if the rays of the setting sun get through the canvas.

Wait in a train station if you're attracted to the stranger, but learn to predict and detect outages; become an experienced conductor, become a skillful knitter, a switching technician (all this in six sessions thanks to the practical new section "Initiation to loco-emotionality") before crossing the steel with luck. Lie down elsewhere than the tracks if your stockings are not of the best quality; everyone knows the power of mimicry (statistics prove it: beautiful features give birth to exclamation points, bean counters, tomatoes, etc.). Despite this, don't lie down on the rails; the train will stop without your consent, he's used to it, you aren't.

Soyez vive, teintée de joie sincère (choisissez vos couleurs avec le même art que vous choisissez votre personnalité hebdromadaire) ayez toujours une tasse de café à portée de la main car, ne l'oubliez pas, pour l'homme l'heure du café est permanente.

Si vous attendez dans un restaurant: Sacrifiez ce rendez-vous. Soyez ailleurs. Un affamé est mieux défendu qu'un blockhaus.

S'il faut attendre à la mairie? À la maison? Vous êtes majeure? Bonne à marier? Bonne à tout faire? Sinon, attendez de l'être avant de parler mariage.

N'attendez pas dans les rues: de véritables petits voyous vous entraîneront loin d'aujourd'hui et où seront alors les beaux atours de vos tares?

Attendez-le au coeur du conflit parmi les feuilles roussies et les vapeurs caramel de vos discrimination. Dissimulez votre voracité sous un sourire semi-lunaire (se trouve dans les tailles suivantes : 42, 43, 44) et surtout arborez une poitrine frileuse; il faut éviter l'insatisfaction chez le partenaire, elle confond les valeurs et aigrit le caractère. Soyez sûre de sa cause. Adoptez une attitude radicalement opposée à celle que vous avez coutume de prendre au lit. Soyez lisse comme une veuve aux mœurs rigides. Isolée et maussade. Et consolez-vous si vous ne savez comment amorcer votre attente: celles qui ne sauraient être fidèles peuvent être pratiques, *mais* hâtez-vous dans ce cas car les places sont rares et derrière le balai, implacable, la mort se dessine.

Be alive, tinged with sincere joy (choose your colors with the same craft you choose your humpdaily personality) always have a cup of coffee on hand because, never forget, for men, coffee time is permanent.

If you wait in a restaurant: give up this rendez-vous. Be elsewhere. A starving man is more impenetrable than a blockhouse.

If you must wait at city hall? At home? Are you of age? Wife material? Housekeeping material? If not, wait to become it before broaching the topic of marriage.

Don't wait in the streets: Little vandals will drag you far from today and what will become of all your dressed up flaws?

Wait for the heart of the conflict amongst the reddened leaves and the caramel fumes of your discriminations. Hide your voracity under a half moon smile (it can be found in the following sizes: 42, 43, 44) and above all bear a nippy chest; a dissatisfied partner must be avoided, as it confuses values and sours the temperament. Be certain of his cause. Adopt a demeanor radically different from the one you assume in bed. Isolated and morose. And comfort yourself if you don't know how to begin your wait: those who do not know how to be faithful can be practical, *but* in that case make haste because spots are scarce and behind the broom, relentlessly, death looms.

CE QUI SE PORTE CET HIVER

La Graisse:

1. *Sur les cuisses*. Celles-ci font une entrée triomphale; nodulées, minau-dantes, frauduleuses, elles arracheraient le cœur du plus insensible. Aussi bien à sept heures en tête à tête avec un homme pressé, mobiles, molletonnées sous une jupe de mousseline, que dans l'autobus à midi vos cuisses doivent être d'attaque. Les jours de soleil, étalez sur les bas-côtés un léger duvet blond (les très brunes se tiendront, les rousses por-teront des moumoutes) et marchez au pas avec le diable.

2. *Sur le ventre*. Tout homme aspire à épouser sa mère; il se souvient avec nostalgie de sa bonne chair, de ses bourrelets, de son bedon.

> *Vous voulez séduire le fils?*
> *Ressemblez à la mère*
> *Mangez pâtes, beurre et pommes de terre*
> *La femme haricot est à l'eau*
> *Vous qui êtes sans repartie*
> *Bourrez votre croupe de soupe et de crème*
> *Vous aurez ainsi le mot ultime*
> *Vous serez grosse, mais sublime.*

Les robes dites "Empire" flattent la poitrine. C'est un fait, mais celle-ci, doux échafaudage de nylon-mousse et de neige, a besoin d'un support: respirez à fond, jetez graine, ceinture, pudeur, et poussez votre ventre en avant tel un général son armée. Sait-on jamais, peut-être est-ce vous la future Joséphine!

80

WHAT TO WEAR THIS WINTER

Fat:

1. *On the thighs.* These will make a triumphant entrance; nodulated, simpering, fraudulent, they will tug at the heartstrings of the most insensitive. To be worn in an after-work tête à tête with a man in a hurry, versatile, stuffed under a muslin skirt, or in a bus at noon your thighs should be at the ready. On sunny days, spread a light blond duvet on the lower sides (those with darker hair will bleach, redheads can wear toupees) and walk in step with the devil.

2. *On the belly.* Every man aspires to marry his mother; he fondly remembers her nice flesh, her love handles, and her paunch.

> *You want to seduce the son?*
> *Look like his mother*
> *Eat pasta, butter and potatoes*
> *The bean lady is a flop*
> *You who have no wit*
> *Stuff your bottom with soup and cream*
> *You will have the last word*
> *You will be fat, but sublime.*

"Empire" dresses bring out the chest. It's a fact, but this soft scaffold of snow and foam padding needs support: breathe deeply, drop the girdle, belt, modesty, and thrust your belly forward as a general would his army. One never knows, perhaps you will be the next Joséphine!

Les chignons:
Mlle X de Rennes nous écrit:
Vite, une coiffure du soir
Vite, une chance d'être mère

Nous répondons:
Mademoiselle
Portez un gros chignon
Vous économiserez du savon
Le savon use la peau, fripe, détend, éduque,
Les rature des la vie autour de vos beaux yeux
Portez une rose dans votre chignon
Vous n'aurez plus honte de votre nuque.
Oui, laissez pousser vos cheveux
Vous ne reconnaîtrez plus votre profil hideux.

Chignons:
Mlle X from Rennes writes:
Quick, an evening hairdo
Quick, a chance to be a mother

We say:
Mademoiselle,
Wear a large bun in your hair
You will save on soap
Soap wears out the skin, ruffles, relaxes, instructs,
Life's mistakes around your beautiful eyes
Carry a rose in your chignon
You'll no longer be ashamed of your neck.
Yes, let your hair grow long
You won't recognize your hideous profile.

CE QUI NE SE PORTE PAS CET HIVER

Les matraques, les bateaux mouches
Les cerfs-volants, les saintes nitouches.

WHAT NOT TO WEAR THIS WINTER

Clubs, tourist boats
Kites, goody two shoes.

CONSEILS D'UNE CONSŒUR

Comment épouser un roi?—Fréquentez la cour.

Votre fils pleure la nuit quand vos amis vous déshabillent?—Achetez la pile Albert, elle ne s'allume qu'une seule fois et tue quand on s'en sert.

ADVICE FROM A SISTER

How to marry a king?—Frequent the court.

Your son cries at night when your friends undress you?—Buy the Albert battery, it only turns on once and kills when it's used.

RHABDOMANCIE

Votre mari vous néglige?
Invitez sa mère à passer la nuit dans votre chambre
Puis affalée dans l'armoire près du lit
Projetez votre oméga plus une poignée de salamandres
Dans le miroir où l'ombre se dandine
Votre mari vous échappe?
Le céleste directeur a besoin d'un régime
Urinez dans sa soupe quand heureux près de vous il s'allonge

Soyez douce mais habile à farcir l'oie grasse
De poulpes de messages
Et de poils de mandragore
Taquinez ses penchants avec un blaireau de soie
Saupoudrez son phalène de sang et de suie
Et surtout souriez quand dans vos bras il se meurt
Malgré lui c'est à vous qu'il pensera

•

Je ne connais pas l'enfer
Mais mon corps brûle depuis ma naissance
Aucun diable n'attise ma haine
Aucun satyre ne me poursuit
Mais le verbe se transforme en vermine entre mes lèvres
Et mon pubis trop sensible à la pluie

DOWSING

Husband neglecting you?
Invite his mother to sleep in your room
Then sprawled in the armoire next to the bed
Project your final word along with a handful of salamanders
In the mirror where the shadow sways
Husband avoiding you?
The divine director must be put on a diet
Piss in his soup when he lies down happily next to you

Be gentle but skillful stuffing the fat goose
With octopus messages
And mandrake roots
Tease his kinks with a silk brush
Sprinkle his moth with blood and soot
Be sure to smile when he dies in your arms
Despite himself he will think of you

        •

I do not know hell
But my body has been burning ever since I was born
No devil stirs my hate
No satyr pursues me
But the verb turns to vermin between my lips
And my pubis too sensitive to the rain

Immobile comme un mollusque flatulent de musique
Se cramponne au téléphone
Et pleure
Malgré moi ma charogne fanatise avec ton vieux sexe débusqué
Qui dort

Motionless like a mollusk flatulent with music
Clings to the telephone
And cries
In spite of myself my carrion fanaticizes over your ousted old cock
That sleeps

CHANT ARABE

L'œil bascule dans la nuit au moment du trépas
O la blanche fulgurante folie des ailes qu'on ne connaît pas
Ouatées de silence elles frôlent le bras sur l'oreiller
Et ouvrent l'œil rond à la nuit de l'impalpable
Le froid tisseur de tubéreuses trépigne sur ma pupille
Je vois glisser la tenture mobile de l'horizon qui rutile et qui s'agite
Telle une peau frémissante sur un corps qui se dérobe
La houle feutrée de mon abdomen se fige de peur démente

J'éternue mais je ne bouge pas
Et l'œil qui cloître mes rêves qui nage et qui clignote
L'œil envahit mes nuits
La nuit la nuit l'orage
L'œil éblouissant aux floraisons étranges
L'œil malade d'images.

ARAB SONG

The eye shifts in the night when death arrives
O the white dazzling madness of wings we will never wear
Padded with silence they brush against the arm on the pillow
And open a round eye to the night of the impalpable
The cold woven tuberoses wait on my pupil
I see the moving wallpaper of the horizon shining and restless
Like the quivering skin on a body revealing itself
The hushed swell of my abdomen braces with a twisted fear

I sneeze but do not move
And the eye that cloisters my dreams swims and signals
The eye that invades my nights
The night the night the storm
The blinding eye with strange blooms
The eye sick with images.

DANS L'OBSCURITÉ À GAUCHE

Pourquoi mes jambes
Autour de ton cou
Cravate collante bouffante bleu foncé
Monotone vestibule de la crique rieuse
Blanches olives de la chrétienté
Pourquoi attendrais-je devant une porte close
Suppliante et timide torride violoncelle
Ayez des enfants
Imbibez vos gencives de vinaigres rares
La plus tendre blancheur est teintée de noir
Votre pénis est plus doux
Que les faciès d'une vierge
Plus irritant que la pitié
Plumitif outil de l'incroyable tohu-bohu
Adieu au revoir c'est fini good-bye
L'envie au mirobolantes floraisons est tarie
Reviendront
Plus vifs plus violentes
Ces mauves bonbons aux pâmoisons dévotes
Pressantes et tétaniques
Les cauchemars véhéments de l'après-midi
Sans toi

IN THE DARK TO THE LEFT

How come my legs
Around your neck
Clinging dark blue bulging necktie
Monotonous foyer of the laughing slit
White olives of Christianity
Why would I wait in front of a closed door
Shy and pleading steamy cello
Have children
Drench your gums in rare vinegar
The most tender white is tinted with black
Your dick is softer
Than the face of a virgin
More irritating than pity
Scribbling tool of this incredible hurly-burly
Good-bye so long it's finished adieu
The craving for unbelievable blossoms has run dry
Will return
More vivid more violent
Those purple sweets of swooning devotees
Pressing and lock jawed
Fierce nightmares of the afternoon
Without you

LÉGER COMME UNE NAVETTE
LE DÉSIR

Pourquoi pleurer sur le crâne chauve de l'ennui

Odieux ou autrement

Esthétique

Raisonneur

Ennui à la française

Je sais fort bien coudre des faux cils à mes paupières

L'agate chasse la haine dans la pâleur d'un regard

Je sais pasticher l'ombre qui ferme les portes

Quand l'amour

Claque des lèvres debout dans le couloir

En relisant tes lettres je pense à nos promenades

Les promesses de l'été qui tardent place Dauphine

Bâillent sous cloche

Il est déjà cinq heures

Partis les cerfs-volants les sages pavés l'imprudence poussière

Brouillé le parterre quadrillé comme un mouchoir

Enlisé le regard lascif

La laine s'entasse sur la patère

La nuit gargouille inerte

Beau désordre sur ma table

Pourquoi pleurer au-dessus d'un baquet de sang

Pourquoi fourrager entre les cuisses du vieux

Venise

Je suis prête à vous couvrir

De ma langue trémière de mon doux bocage

LIGHT AS A SHUTTLE DESIRE

Why weep on the bald head of boredom
Heinous or otherwise
Esthetic
Reasoner
Ennui à la French
I'm an expert in sewing false eyelashes to my eyelids
The agate banishes hate in the paleness of a glance
I know how to weave the shadow that closes doors
When love
Smacks its lips standing in the hallway
Rereading your letters I think of our walks
The promises of summer lingering at Place Dauphine
Yawning beneath the bells
It's already five o'clock
Gone are the kites the wise cobblestones the careless dust
The scrambled floor tiled like a handkerchief
Entangled and lascivious glance
The wool piles up on the coat hook
The sluggish night gargles
Handsome mess on my table
Why cry over a banquet of blood
Why rummage between the thighs of the old man
Venice
I am ready to cover you
With my hollyhock tongue of my soft hedges

Prête à ciseler mon pelage
Voler chez les boutiquières
Sauter le fossé sans jupons ni œillères
Pour sombrer encore humide entre tes bras de pacotille
Pourquoi surnager se maquiller se divertir
Pourquoi répondre
Pourquoi fuir
Le souvenir de ton sommeil glacé
Me suit pas à pas
Quand pourrai-je te revoir
Sans verser des larmes sur moi

Ready to chisel my fur
Stolen from the shopkeepers
Jump the ditch without petticoats or blinders
To fall still moist into your arms of rubbish
Why float put on makeup have fun
Why answer
Why run
The memory of your frozen sleep
Follows me step by step
When can I see you again
Without shedding tears on myself

L'APPEL AMER D'UN SANGLOT

Venez femmes aux seins fébriles
Écouter en silence le cri de la vipère
Et sonder avec moi le bas brouillard roux
Qui enfle soudain la voix de l'ami
La rivière est fraîche autour de son corps
Sa chemise flotte blanche comme la fin d'un discours
Dans l'air substantiel avare de coquillages
Inclinez-vous filles intempestives
Abandonnez vos pensées à capuchon
Vos sottes mouillures vos bottines rapides
Un remous s'est produit dans la végétation
Et l'homme s'est noyé dans la liqueur

THE BITTER CALL OF TEARS

Come women with feverish breasts
Listen in silence to the viper's scream
And probe with me the low red fog
That suddenly swells the voice of the friend
The river is cool around his body
His white shirt floating like the end of a speech
In the expansive air emptied of seashells
Take a bow untimely ladies
Forget your hooded thoughts
Your foolish moistness your quick booties
An eddy took shape in the plants
And man drowned himself in liquor

DANS LE SILLAGE DU MONT-ARBOIS

Je pense à ce petit morceau d'anguille
Chair verdâtre sous le vernis blanc
De ta façade
Flamme rouge entre mes cuisses
Quand à genou dans la neige
J'arrose nos pas de mes larmes tardives
Je pense à l'été gardien de musée
Aux fleurs brunies de mon ventre
À l'asphodèle sous le corail de me fesses
Dormantes
À tous les jouets que j'ai cassés dans ma fuite
Ci-gît Juillet mois de la longue plume
Tendresse de l'azur toute méditerranéenne
Manchette babillarde du désert
Comment avale-t-on l'indifférence et la peste
Ma bouche se veut tombe mais ne sais pas mentir
Triste vacarme du dégel dans l'obscurité bovine
Sperme de boudin sur la page puérile
L'hiver
Je pense à mon amour et mes yeux distillent Mercuria
Bec de gaz fuligineux
Seringue de la dernière marche
Seule ma bouche se défend et te suffit
Seule ma bouche te gaspille

IN THE WAKE OF MONT-ARBOIS

I think of that little piece of eel
Greenish flesh under the white varnish
Of your façade
Red flame between my thighs
When kneeling in the snow
I water our footsteps with my belated tears
I think of the summer guardian of museums
To the browned flowers of my belly
To the asphodel under the coral of my bum
Sleeping
To all the toys I broke in my escape
Here lies July month of the long feather
Tenderness of the sky fully Mediterranean
Talkative headline of the desert
How does one swallow indifference and plague
My mouth would be a grave but does not know how to lie
Sad upheaval of the thaw in the bovine darkness
Sperm of black pudding on a childish beach
Winter
I think of my love and my eyes distill Mercuria
Sooty gas burner
Syringe of the last step
Only my mouth defends itself and satisfies you
Only my mouth wastes you

NUIT DE VEILLE DANS UNE CELLULE EN CRISTAL DE ROCHE

Être invisible et aimée de vous
Nocturne oiseau de proie
Je plane derrière la porte pluvieuse
Solitaire et sauvage
Lourde
De la gélatineuse souffrance orientale

Courir rouge de votre odeur
Dans le jeu phosphorescent des vagues
Nue rousse et tentaculaire
Suspendue au cri de la petite flûte
Pétale
Mon pubis se soulève
Calme houle calme calme
Malheureuse que je suis
La lune brise l'image engloutie
Avant même que sur le sable rose
Votre tête puisse venir mourir

Être invisible et aimée de vous
À quelques lieues de l'Atlantide
Sur la mer ouverte de mes songes

SLEEPLESS NIGHTS IN A CELL OF ROCK CRYSTAL

To be invisible and loved by you
Nocturnal bird of prey
I hover behind the rainy door
Alone and wild
Heavy
With that viscous oriental suffering

Running red from your scent
In the phosphorescent play of waves
Naked, redheaded and sprawling
Suspended by the scream of a little flute
Petal
Pubis rising
Calm swell calm calm
Unfortunate that I am
The moon breaks the immersed image
Even before your head can come
To die on the pink sand

To be invisible and loved by you
A few leagues from Atlantis
On the open waters of my dreams

LE SOLEIL DANS LE CAPRICORNE

Trois jours de repos
Pourquoi pas la tombe
J'étouffe sans ta bouche
L'attente déforme l'aube prochaine
Et les longues heures de l'escalier
Sentent le gaz
À plat ventre j'attends demain
Je vois luire ta peau
Dans la grande trouée de la nuit
Le balancement lent d'un beau clair de lune
Sur la mer intérieure de mon sexe
Poussière sur poussière
Marteau sur matelas
Soleil sur tambour de plomb
Toujours souriant ta main tonne l'indifférence
Cruellement vêtu incliné vers le vide
Tu dis non et le plus petit objet qu'abrite un corps de femme
Courbe l'échine
Nice artificielle
Parfum factice de l'heure sur le canapé
Pour quelles pâles girafes
Ai-je délaissé Byzance
La solitude pue
Une pierre de lune dans un cadre ovale
Encore une insomnie au jointures rigides

SUN IN CAPRICORN

Three days of rest
Why not the tomb
I can't breathe without your mouth
The wait warps the coming dawn
And the staircase's long hours
Smell of gas
Flat on my stomach I wait for tomorrow
I see your skin gleam
In the great breach of the night
The slow sway of a fine moonlight
On the inland sea of my sex
Dust on dust
Hammer on mattress
Sun on beating drum
Still smiling your hand thunders indifference
Dressed cruelly tilted towards emptiness
You say no and the smallest object housed in a woman's body
Arches the spine
Artificial Nice
False perfume from the hour on the couch
For what pale giraffes
Have I abandoned Byzantium
Loneliness sucks
A moonstone in an oval frame
Yet another insomnia with rigid joints

Encore un poignard palpitant sous la pluie
Diamants et délires du souvenir de demain
Sueurs de taffetas plages sans abri
Démence de ma chair égarée

Yet another dagger pulsing under the rain
Diamonds and deliriums of tomorrow's memories
Taffeta sweat homeless beaches
Madness of my flesh gone astray

SOUVENIR IMPOSÉ PAR LE NORD AU SUD VAINCU

Je vois
Le coteau fleuri qu'est ton ventre
Sur l'oreiller
De la plage
L'hiver
Quand il pleut
Le vaste nombril
Aspire sanglote
Et saigne
Il y a
Des quadrilles de fourmis
Dans mon oreille encombrée de plombs
Apprêtés
De lignes d'hameçons
Et de ce moelleux duvet
Le tabac
Je ne peux écouter qu'à tâtons
L'escargot téléphone
Voix unique
Du désert
Je ne sais goûter qu'à huis clos
Le pâle pétunia du coussin indulgent
Si vite par mes lèvres
Englouti
Pourquoi dois-je souffrir

MEMORIES IMPOSED BY THE NORTH ON A CONQUERED SOUTH

I see
The hillside in bloom that is your belly
On the pillow
Of the beach
Winter
When it's raining
The vast belly button
Sucks sobs
And bleeds
There are
Ant quadrilles
In my ear cluttered with sinkers
Prepared
With hook lines
And of this soft duvet
Tobacco
I can only listen gropingly
The snail is calling
Unique voice
Of the desert
I can only taste behind closed doors
The pale petunia of the indulgent cushion
So quickly by my lips
Swallowed
Why must I suffer

M'embourber ainsi
Entre les haies de soupçons
Les ballons allégoriques
Et les méchancetés de fille
Ô ventre prolifique naïf poulpe
Un peu fade
Raideur narquoise qui vers ma bouche
Chemines
Il y a plus de cailloux que la de terre
Autour d'un mort
Plus de nuits parcourues que de crimes

Bogged down this way
Between hedges and suspicions
Allegorical balloons
And the wickedness of girls
O prolific belly naïve octopus
Somewhat faded
Sardonic stiffness towards my mouth
Snakes
There are more stones than earth
Around a corpse
More nights traveled than crimes

SOUS LA TOUR CENTRALE

Pour Matta

Des mains erraient sur les touches
Et des paroles étranges venaient d'Elle
Flottaient à la surface du ruisseau
J'écoutais le dialecte des sexes qu'on déshabille
Des mains écrivaient sur les vannes
Vingt-quatre heures sur vingt-quatre
Et des assassinats devaient suivre
Dans le même crépuscule bleuâtre où sifflent les serpents d'acier
Où crient les mouettes et s'épanouissent les femmes mûres
Aux pistils enflammés et blessures de pacotille
J'étais un peu intimidée
Ç'aurait été tellement délicieux
De pouvoir uriner dans la rue

UNDER THE CENTRAL TOWER

For Matta

Hands wandered on the keys
And strange words came from Her
Floating to the surface of the creek
I listened to the dialect of undressed sexes
Hands were writing on valves
Twenty-four seven
And assassinations would follow
In the same bluish twilight where steel snakes whistle
Where gulls shriek and mature women blossom
With swollen pistils and cheap wounds
I was a bit intimidated
It would have been so delicious
To piss in the street

FLEURIE COMME LA LUXURE

Tu dis que les femmes
Doivent souffrir se polir et voyager sans perdre haleine
Réveiller les pierreries embellies par le fard
Chanter ou se taire déchirer la brume
Hélas je ne saurais danser dans un marais de sang
Ta figure brille de l'autre côté de la rive heureuse
Tout ce qui est vivant pourrit

Tu dis que les femmes
Doivent savoir se dépouiller de tout même
Du nourrisson encore rétif
À l'amour
Ta figure bleuit à mesure que ta fortune grandit
Et moi je veux mourir vautrée dans la sauge
Orgueilleusement mauvaise dans l'immobilité de l'exil

Tu dis que les femmes
Doivent se détruire pour ne pas enfanter
Et attendre attendre la solide volupté qui serpente
Hélas je n'aime pas faire l'amour sur le tapis
Belzébuth roucoule dans la gorge des pigeons
Ta bague brûle ma cuisse
L'émeraude est la virginité
Du riche

FLOWERED LIKE LEWDNESS

You say that women
Should suffer primping and travel without losing their breath
To wake the precious gems embellished with makeup
To sing or shut up to tear the mist
Alas I would not know how to dance in a swamp of blood
Your shape shines on the other side of the cheerful shore
All that is alive rots

You say that women
Should know how to strip away everything even
The newborn still restless
For love
Your face turns blue as your fortune grows
And I want to die wallowing in sage
Proudly wicked in the stillness of exile

You say that women
Should destroy themselves to avoid childbirth
And wait wait for that solid and snaking delight
Alas I do not like to make love on the carpet
Beelzebub coos in the throat of the pigeons
Your ring burns my thigh
The emerald is the virginity
Of the rich man

Tu dis que les femmes
Sont faites pour nourrir
La fumée repentante qui halète à l'église
Les truies pales et pleines piquées de soies souillées
Les têtes coupées aussi et pourquoi pas après tout
Étonnantes nuits du pôle aux silences sanguinaires
Je crois que maintenant je peux te laisser partir

Tes jambes volent haut dans la sacristie
Claquant
Des genoux
Comme autant de prédicateurs
Je suis bien contente d'avoir un chapeau sur la tête
Même si ton urine contient toute la féerie du mariage
Tu dis que les femmes sont chanoines du délire
Hélas moi je ne savoure que la mort

You say that women
Are made to nurture
The repenting smoke gasping in church
The pale and pregnant sows stitched with soiled silk
Heads chopped too and why not after all
Stunning nights of bloody silence at the pole
I think that I can let you go now

Your legs fly high in the sacristy
Slamming
At the knees
Like so many preachers
I am relieved to have a hat on my head
Even if your piss holds all the fairytales of marriage
You say that women are canons of delirium
As for myself, alas, I only savor death

SÉANCE TENANTE

Pour S.

Tout ceci parce que j'aime faire l'amour sous l'eau
Pommader mes cheveux de brouillard et de bile
Et me laisser aller au fond du canapé
Avec un palefrenier bossu
Et un doigt de vagabondage

Tout ceci parce que tu sais que j'étais voleuse autrefois

RIGHT AWAY
For S.

All of this because I like to make love underwater
Smearing my hair with fog and bile
And let myself go in the depths of the couch
With a hunched stable boy
And a roaming finger

All this because you know I was once a thief

PAPIER D'ARGENT

Je veux vivre à l'ombre de ton visage
Plus hostile que le bois
Plus vigilant que Noé
Penché sur les flots
Je veux creuser des routes dans les lunaires collines
De ton corps
Allumer des feux dans le creux de tes paupières
Savoir te parler et partir quand il est temps
Encore
Je veux vivre lentement dans le jeu de ton décor
Flotter entre mère et père
Tel le sourire de l'écho dans la pénombre
Dévêtue
Être l'étincelle sur l'oreiller
Entendue par le sourd qui se croit seul
Cannibale
Je veux titiller de désespoir sous ta langue
Je veux être lys sur ton ombre légère
Et me coucher éblouie sous l'araignée
Bonne nuit Irène
C'est l'heure

TIN FOIL

I want to live in the shadow of your face
Harsher than the wood
More vigilant than Noah
Tilted towards the waves
I want to dig roads in the lunar hills
Of your body
Light the fire in the pit of your eyelids
To know how to speak with you and leave while there's still time
Left
I want to live slowly in the game of your set
To float between mother and father
As a smile of the echo in twilight
Naked
To be the spark on the pillow
To be heard by the deaf man who thinks he is alone
A cannibal
I want to titillate with despair under your tongue
I want to be the lily on your weightless shadow
And to lay down blinded under the spider
Goodnight Irene
It's time

L'AMOUREUSE GUERRIÈRE

Trois ans dit la mante
Et ainsi qu'une boutonnière lentement entrouverte
Pour se contracter encore en joyeuse spasmodie
Elle sourit
Le fil filé déroule
Dénudant les reins de la hennissante
Tendresse
Trois ans de constructions et saillies solitaires
Seule demeure
L'immense ameublement ébréché
Fier débris inutile
Du tronçon masculin attelé à sa besogne
Échappe-t-il aux pattes ravisseuses
De l'amante
Comme elle je dévorerai celui qui violera mes flancs
Aux pulsations
Barbares
Comme elle je grignoterai mon frère
Il faut savoir attendre pouvoir se venger
Imiter les insectes pour plaire

WOMAN WARRIOR IN LOVE

Three years said the mantis
And like a buttonhole slowly left ajar
So as to tighten again in spastic joy
She smiles
The woven thread unravels
Exposing the loins of a whinnying
Tenderness
Three years of constructions and solitary protrusions
All that remain
Are the massive chipped furnishings
Proud and useless wreckage
Of the masculine section hitched to its labor
Does he escape the ravishing paws
Of the mistress
Like her I would devour the one who might broadside me
With barbarous
Throbs
Like her I would nibble my brother
One must learn to wait to take revenge
Imitate insects in order to please

L'HEURE VELUE

Pourquoi vieillir
Les eaux vives de la déraison coulent sur ton beau visage
Il y a des mots qui se répandent
D'autres qui dressent
Tel l'anathème
Quatre chevaux blancs jaillissent d'une bouteille de lait
Et galopent autour de ta seule extase
Ton rendez-vous manqué de la place de l'Aima
Ton front humide patinoire aux flammes de comédien
Ton nez ta bouche
Ton cœur froid
Les incertitudes du rêve placent un cœur dans ton visage
Tel un arbre sur le pont de la folie clémente
Le bleu se perd dans le noir des maladies incurables
Il fait jour trop tôt pour satisfaire le rêveur
L'insecte remonte les murs raides
Comme demain
Le corset imprégné de sommeil
Et sur les pattes
La boue rubis de la Seine
Pourquoi vieillir
Les odeurs aussi changent de nom
Seul l'amour dans ta bouche a comme un goût de moignon
Qu'y a-t-il donc au point où pénètre le dard
Qui fait mûrir mon cœur bel abcès dans la tombe

THE HAIRY HOUR

Why age
The rushing waters of folly flow across your handsome face
There are words that spread
Others that stand erect
Like the anathema
Four white horses spurt from a milk bottle
And gallop around your one and only pleasure
Your missed connection at the Place de l'Aima
Your moist brow like a skating rink with blazes of an actor
Your nose your mouth
Your cold heart
The uncertainties of the dream place a heart on your face
Like a tree on the verge of mild madness
The blue loses itself in the black of incurable illness
Day dawns too early to please the dreamer
The insect crawls up the steep walls
Like tomorrow
The corset impregnated with sleep
And on its paws
The ruby red mud of the Seine
Why age
Smells also change their names
Only the love in your mouth still tastes like a severed limb
What is in that place penetrated by the dart
That makes my heart ripen beautiful abscess in the tomb

J'ai mal dans chaque pore de mon cerveau acétylène
Chaleur zébrée de mon germe fragile
Pourquoi vieillir loin de toi

I feel pain in every pore of my acetylene brain
Striped heat of my fragile seed
Why age away from you

LA PISTE DU BROUILLARD

De désespoir
Je mangerai la terre
Demain
Le grand chien noir
Obscurcit la lampe
Partie la violette sombre aux pommettes spatulées
Partie l'étoile oisive des plaines gonflées de pluie
L'abeille cherche l'épingle au tréfonds de mon regard
Midi
Ma pupille éclate sur la berge
L'arc-en-ciel de l'orgasme se reflète au plafond
Sous tes genoux serrés mon oeil
S'ossifie
Dans ton sommeil oblique
Une végétation d'étain
Prend feu
Et puis c'est toute l'orbite
Qui se vide dans ma main
Pourquoi ne prendrais-je pas une virgule pour un cœur
La rue n'est que masturbation
De femme

THE PATH OF FOG

In despair
I would eat the earth
Tomorrow
The big black dog
Darkens the lamp
Gone is the dark violet with flattened cheekbones
Gone is the idle star of the plains bloated with rain
The bee looks for the needle in the depths of my gaze
Noon
The pupil of my eye bursts on the riverbank
The rainbow of orgasm is reflected on the ceiling
Under your tucked knees my eye
Ossifies
In your oblique sleep
A tin greenery
Catches fire
And it's the entire orbit
That empties in my hand
Why would I not take a comma for a heart
The street is nothing more than the masturbation
Of women

LA FAÇADE DE L'OBSESSION

Dis religieux
Puis-je mettre oreille à terre
Planter dans la ouate chauvine ma terreur et mon ennui
Rêver tout haut le bruit du serpent dans ma fente
Quitter la vie ainsi qu'un émigré fuit le pays du plus grand cercueil
Puis-je interdire ma porte à la fière somnambule
Et forcer ses yeux oblongs à se vider dans la citerne
Telles des minutes dans la tombe
Puis-je croiser le fer avec la lycose enguirlandée
Détruire la vue lointaine des glaïeuls utérins
Ou empêcher une seule phrase de violer mon esprit
Réponds religieux
Sous le soleil bigle de Tolède
La peau enflée de nos retrouvailles
Se fendille
Et si sous la table ta main chaude cherche la mienne
Puis-je pisser tout mon soûl pour autant

THE FACE OF OBSESSION

Tell me Religious
Can I place my ear to the ground
Plant in the chauvinistic cotton wool my terror and ennui
Dreaming out loud the sound of the snake in my crotch
To leave life as an emigré flees the country of the largest coffin
Can I forbid my door to the proud sleepwalker
And force her oblong eyes to empty in the cistern
Like minutes in a tomb
Can I cross blades with the festooned wolf spider
Destroy the distant view of uterine gladiolas
Or stop a single sentence from violating my spirit
Answer Religious
Under the cockeyed sun of Toledo
The swollen skin of our reunion
Cracks
And if under the table your warm hand searches for mine
May I just as well piss to my heart's content

HEUREUX LES ÉTOURDIS

Heureux les faméliques
Les enfantins les prolifiques
Heureux ceux à qui le ventre ordonne
Sacrifices vils désespoirs
Et voluptés secrètes
Ils connaîtront d'autres planètes
Justes colères vertes futaies
Et corbeilles de poisons
Heureux les maléfiques
Aux doigts d'airain et bouches de suie
Heureux les piliers bourrés de chair grasse
Heureux ceux qui savent pénétrer l'avenir par le toit
Sans attirer l'attention du canon monacal
Aux chuchotements agglutinés
Et mesquines morsures de chien
Heureux les serviteurs du silence supérieur
L'amour n'a que faire de l'anonymat
Dieu laisse son fusil à l'église

HAPPY ARE THE STUNNED

Happy are the starved
The childish the prolific
Blessed are those whom the belly orders
Sacrifices vile despairs
And secret delights
They will know other planets
Righteous rages green plantations
And baskets of poison
Blessed are the evil ones
With fingers of bronze and mouths of soot
Happy the pillars stuffed with fatty flesh
Blessed are those who know how to pierce the future through the roof
Without attracting the attention of the monastic canon
To agglutinated whispers
And petty dog bites
Blessed are the servants of the mighty silence
Love cares not for anonymity
God leaves his gun at church

DES MYRIADS D'AUTRES MORTS

La nuit gorgée d'étoiles
S'étend sur la forêt
Je dors les yeux ouverts fascinée par le mur
Je connais tant de ruses
De bosquets d'asphodèles aux longs pistils sonores
Prêts à toute éventualité armés pour me plaire
Tant de blessures émeraude
Tant d'actions coupables aux noms oubliés
Tant de soleils démasqués
Sinistres bâilleurs dans la brume
Qui attendent l'heure unique pour plonger
La nuit je suis soumise
Happée par le gouffre aux hallalis barbares
Je quitte mon foyer
Heureuse de fuir le théâtre historique
De rejeter mes robes froissées par trop de mains hâtives
Mes convictions mêmes et leurs grilles étincelantes
J'oublie
Je n'attends plus l'affection vulgaire
Je traverse lunes déserts lacs
Je suis l'animal de la nuit
Folle dit l'homme
En rêvant ainsi
Tu perdras ton diamant
Les couloirs de l'espace

A MYRIAD OF MORE DEATHS

The star-filled night
Extends over the forest
I sleep with open eyes fascinated by the wall
I know so many tricks
Of thickets of asphodels with long resonant pistils
Ready for anything armed to please me
So many emerald wounds
So many guilty actions with forgotten names
So many unmasked suns
Ominous yawners in the mist
Who wait for the single hour to dive
At night I submit
Caught in the abyss with the barbaric kill
I leave my home
Happy to escape the historic stage
To throw away my dresses crumpled by too many hasty hands
Even my convictions and their shining grids
I forget
I no longer wait for vulgar affection
I cross moons deserts lakes
I am the animal of the night
Madness says the man
To dream like this
You will lose your diamond
The corridors of space

Peuplés de formes ultimes
Pétrissent le somnambule
Et se nourrissent de sa chair
Tu verras ton noir pubis épinglé sur le roc diagonal
Folle décoiffée par la hideuse puanteur
Tu mourras dans l'abîme
J'aime rôder la nuit
Tomber de haut sur un marchand de pierres
L'égorger et boire
Le son délicieusement accentué de sa voix
Écoute
Les damnés sont à table dans leurs tristes habitacles de verre
J'aime décourager
À l'aube une vieille carpe prend le relais
Le ciel soulève sa poitrine aux boutons de nacre
Je m'endors pour de bon sur mon oreiller colossal
Un filet de sang ternit l'émeri du lapidaire
La grande bouche verticale
Annonce que c'est demain

Filled with final forms
Who knead the sleepwalker
And feed on his flesh
You'll see your black pubis pinned to the diagonal rock
Madwoman disheveled by the awful stench
You will die in the abyss
I like to prowl at night
Fall from above on a stone vendor
To slit his throat and drink
The delicious accent of his voice
Listen
The damned are at the table in their pathetic glass cabins
I like to discourage
At dawn an old carp takes over
The sky lifts its mother-of-pearl button chest
I fall asleep for good on my colossal pillow
A trickle of blood tarnishes the emery of the lapidary
The large vertical mouth
Announces tomorrow is here

SONNE N'ÉCOUTE PERSONNE N'ÉCOUTE PER

Fulgurants sauvages chevaux d'Europe
Chaos de membres brisés
Murs mouvants
Soleils
Pavés sanguinolents lancés par des mains aveugles
Dans la mayonnaise
Dans la boue
Dans l'égout familièrement béant
Dans tout ce qui se nomme et qui n'ose se montrer
L'Arabe en moi grelotte sur chaque marche de chair
Soumise
Capable d'attendre longtemps la triste mâture promise
Saluez ô mes amis la mort ses fuites ses fusions
Pour elle seule il n'est guère de zone interdite
Dans le brasier de l'amour passion
Puis
Une fois la nuit venue
La nuit la nuit l'orage
Je reviens vers ma jeunesse
Le phosphore effréné
La chaleur bestiale
Les vagues de la vengeance permise
Le sable
Le bâillement de la nuit fragile
L'éther

ONE LISTEN TO NO ONE LISTEN TO NO

Dazzling wild horses of Europe
Chaos of broken limbs
Moving walls
Suns
Bloody cobblestones thrown by the hands of the blind
Into mayonnaise
Into mud
Into the familiarly gaping sewer
Into everything with a name that doesn't dare show itself
The Arab in me shudders on every step of flesh
Submitted
Able to wait a long time for the sad promised masts
O my friends, salute death her leaks her fusions
For her only are there no forbidden places
In the blaze of love's passion
And then
Once the night has fallen
The night the night the storm
I return to my youth
The unbridled phosphorous
The brutish heat
The waves of permitted revenge
The sand
The yawning of the fragile night
Ether

À l'heure où Paris s'allume
L'animal libre court encore sous nos phares
L'âme exquise
Là-bas sur la route sexe subtil du désert
La belle pomme voilée ne vomit plus son ver
Clair de lune
Je suis juive il est vrai
Capable d'apprendre la liberté dans la rue
Où l'infamie fait étalage
Je maudis en moi la femme qui accepte
La face triangulaire du cadenas
Silence
Je crache sur ceux qui écoutent
Derrière leurs prunelles limpides
Leurs braguettes piétinées par trop de cerveaux fêlés
Leurs portes salement closes
Nomenclature du cauchemar
Une seule goutte d'urine sur le trottoir
Tous les museaux s'allongent

At the hour when Paris switches on
The free animal still runs under our headlights
Exquisite soul
Over there on the road subtle sex of the desert
The beautiful veiled apple no longer vomits her worm
Moonlight
I am Jewish, this is true
Able to learn freedom in the street
Where infamy is on display
I curse the woman in me who accepts
The triangular face of the lock
Silence
I spit on those who listen
Behind the clear pupil of their eyes
Their fly trampled on by too many cracked brains
Their doors filthily closed
Nomenclature of nightmares
One drop of urine on the sidewalk
Every nose snouts about

AU-DELÀ DE LA HOULE

J'interromps ici la nuit douloureuse
Des nuages venant de Belgrade
Défilent sous la coupole
Et les différents alliages du fer et de l'acier
Tournent mystérieusement leurs aiguilles
Vers le jouet
Qui menace l'air glacial de sa verge
Peut-être deviendrai-je folle
Délabrée comme une cuvette ou un vieux nid
D'Arabe
Mes allumettes diminuent
Personne ne se soucie de ma très grande détresse
Et le nom de ma coiffe
Est British
Est-ce qu'il neige sur Londres monsieur Herbie
Le jour blafard fait les cent pas sur le mur
Un claquement de diaphragme ponctue mes fêtes intimes
Ta langue perce des meurtrières dans les cloisons de mon coffre-fort
Ta langue au pataugements de pudding
Et rythme humide
De nabot
La lueur d'un fanal au-dessus de mon matelas
Telle l'œillade de la lune sur la soie d'un paysage blanc
Dessine des marches dans les ruines
Qui jonchent les sables de mes vastes pupilles

BEYOND THE SWELL

I interrupt here the painful night
Clouds from Belgrade
Parade beneath the church dome
And the different alliances of iron and steel
Mysteriously turn their needles
Towards the toy
That threatens the frigid air of its penis
Perhaps I will become mad
In disrepair like a toilet bowl or an old nest
Of an Arab
My matches are dwindling
No one cares for my great despair
And the name of my hairdo
Is British
Is it snowing in London mister Herbie
The pale day paces on the wall
A snapping of the diaphragm punctuates my intimate parties
Your tongue pierces the embrasures in the walls of my vault
Your tongue wading in pudding
And moist rhythm
Of a dwarf
The glow of a lantern above my mattress
Like the glance of the moon on the silk of a white landscape
Draws steps in the ruins
That line the sands of the pupils of my eyes

Bien des demeures portent lunettes

La nuit

J'ai sangloté sur ton épaule autrefois

Tu disais

Tu te trompes secoue-toi

Tu te trompes très sûrement

Tu ne cessais d'osciller sur tes irritantes béquilles

Et l'énorme balancier de ton rire Fracassa le tympan de l'horloge

J'avais faim cet après-midi-là

Et envie de pleurer

D'inonder le parquet de frémissantes marquises

Aux diadèmes de saphir et crinolines de diaphanes

Aux pieds mouillés et hoquets discordants

Un mot vibre dans le silence de ma tombe

Voyage

Personne n'écoute de toute façon

Une main verte surgit de l'édredon discret

Encombré de poissons aux longs becs

Charognards

Puis un bras une chandelle

Un réverbère indécis

Vrai tumulte de miroirs sur la surface glauque de mon sein

Pourquoi ne m'appelles-tu pas

Je projette ma poitrine

Sur les tours de Notre-Dame

La crème fouettée de l'orgasme

Tamise l'éclairage rôti de Saint-Sulpice

Les remparts les créneaux Tourelles et décorations

Du désert volcanique dépouillé de sa chair

Basculent au bord de la marmite panique

La barre d'appui cède

Many homes wear glasses
At night
I used to sob on your shoulder
You would say
You're wrong get a grip
You're wrong most certainly
You wouldn't stop swaying on your annoying crutches
And the massive pendulum of your laugh
Broke the eardrum of the clock
I was hungry that afternoon
And wanted to cry
To flood the floor with trembling marquises
With sapphire diadems and see-through crinolines
With wet feet and discordant hiccups

One word vibrates in the silence of my tomb
Travel
No one is listening anyway
A green hand appears from the subtle duvet
Weighed down by fish with long beaks
Scavenging
Then an arm a candle
An indecisive headlight
A real uproar of mirrors on the sleazy surface of my breast
Why don't you call me
I project my chest
On the towers of Notre-Dame
The whipped cream of orgasm
Softens the roasted light of Saint-Sulpice
The battlements the crenels the Turrets and decorations
Of the volcanic desert shorn of its flesh
Tipping on the edge of the pot of panic
The handrail yields

Le plus terrible des serpents mord sa langue pour ne pas crier
Les cheminées noires s'enroulent en spirales autour de la colline
Jaune-orange sous ses hardes automnales
Mais peut-être te verrai-je lundi
En chair et en os dans le vide séraphique d'un bouleau sous la neige
Mes bras se crispent sur leurs gonds
Je vois fleurir l'éternuement
Dans le gosier amorphe du pistolet scolaire
Sur la vitre
Un long doigt de brouillard
Traîne son haleine
Entre les cavaliers de la propagande
Et le radeau de *la Méduse*
Je sème mes yeux à tout vent
Sur les eaux basses du pur ennui
Au jardin où les pétunias voguent à la dérive
Têtes folles de l'été qui ne se savent pas vaincues
Dans chaque recoin du quartier des bons pugilistes dans le sucre épars au
    plafond
Du matin
La girafe enfarinée se dresse nue sur ses sabots
Le cigare tombe en loques là sur le lavabo
Tu connais Georges crie la ville
Rappelle-toi le soleil de Nonza
J'entonne une rengaine
Aux rondelles de saucisson
Et pastilles de haute mer
Arrêt casse-croûte dans la glacière de février
Une colonne de poussière masque mon enfance
De sa vaine palissade
Il n'est jamais minuit à la Gare Centrale
Personne ne prend plus le train pour Venise
Je suis toujours rivée au même point de l'indifférence

The most terrible of snakes bites its tongue so as not to scream
The black chimneys spiral around the hill
Yellow-orange under its fall herds
But perhaps I will see you on Monday
In the flesh in the seraphic void of a birch tree under the snow
My arms stiffen in their hinges
I see the sneeze in bloom
In the sluggish throat of the school pistol
In the window
A long finger in the fog
Drags its breath
Between the horsemen of propaganda
And the frigate of *La Méduse*
I sow my eyes to all winds
In the shallow waters of pure boredom
In the garden where petunias sail adrift
Mad minds of summer who don't yet know they've been defeated
In every corner of the neighborhood good fighters in the sugar scattered
    on the ceiling
Of the morning
The floured giraffe stands naked on her hind hooves
The cigar falls to pieces there on the sink
You know George yells the city
Remember the sun of Nonza
I sing the first notes of an old tune
Of sausage slices
And open sea lozenges
Snack stop in the icehouse of February
A column of dust masks my childhood
From its vain palisade
It is never past midnight at the Central Station
No one takes the train to Venice anymore
I am always riveted to the same point of indifference

Fratres semper
Pourtant il est bon de se sentir fertile
Dans l'archipel malais
De partir en fumée comme une bûche sifflante et chaude
Sur ton épaule de ciel bleu chauve de souvenirs
Prélunaires
Je porte en moi un peuple ancien
Ils émergent dans mes rêves
Barbus et pauvres armés de cérémonies
Tabernacles ambulants
Leurs femmes me ressemblent sous leurs voiles onduleux
Leurs enfants paisibles et sombres tirent l'avenir par la queue
Dolente neige qui couvre mon coeur gelé
Je suis la crête du vallonnement vert-de-gris
Dernière-née d'une clôture de fil de fer
Et d'un hennissement d'ébène
Je pressens quelquefois l'abominable abîme
Aux profondeurs édentées
À la lubricité de chienne
Je viens vers toi riante et sereine
Sans fausse note
Ni accent mal placé dans le nombril
Habitée par le chant narcissique des grandes orgues
Je m'étends
Sur ta coquille labyrinthique
Je t'écrase
J'arrache les plaisantes Japonaises de tes murs
Je bois ton urine comme du miel
Je bave sur la pierre tombale de ta très belle salle de bains
Aux fleurs de lotus et expressions musicales
Je me sauve à toutes jambes sur l'ardoise de ton passage
tu ne fais plus partie de ma vie
Venimeuse pensée

Fratres semper
And yet it is good to feel fertile
In the Malaysian archipelago
To go up in smoke like a hot whistling log
On your shoulder of blue sky bald of memories
Pre-lunar
I carry in me an ancient people
They appear in my dreams
Bearded and poor armed with ceremonies
Traveling tabernacles
Their women look like me under their billowing veils
Their children peaceful and gloomy pull the future with their tails
Sorrowful snow that covers my frozen heart
I am the crest of green-gray hills
Last born of a barbed wire fence
And of an ebony whinny
I sometimes foresee the abominable abyss
Of toothless depths
Of dog lechery
I come towards you laughing and serene
Without any wrong notes
Nor misplaced accent in the belly button
Filled with the narcissistic song of great organs
I stretch out
On your labyrinthine shell
I crush you
I rip the pleasant Japanese women from your walls
I drink your urine like honey
I drool on the tomblike stone of your beautiful bathroom
Of lotus flowers and musical expressions
I escape as fast as I can on the slate of your crossing
You are no longer part of my life
Poisonous thought

Je ne suis plus qu'une image sur l'arrière-train
du serpent travail
La Femme Orientale du récit.

I am nothing more than an image on the backside
Of the working snake
A narrative's Oriental Woman.

MINUIT À PERTE DE VUE

Enfin des nouvelles
L'eau resplendissante crie hosanna
Mes yeux disparaissent
Par à-coups
Oui par spasmes
Happés par la candeur
De l'onde

Les puissances d'erreur
Arpentent le terrain
Qui borde les deux rives
Sagesse étroite
Des cosaques
Aux blessures brasillantes
De vitraux

J'attends la faucille
Et le beau paulownia dans mon jardin saccagé
Ceint le ciel de ses feuillages sonores
Telle est la sagesse de l'ombre
La femme hurla
Pourquoi cacher tes seins
L'eau ne saurait œuvrer
Que dans l'absurde
Laisse-moi souffler sur leurs pointes précises

ENDLESSLY MIDNIGHT

Finally news from the river
The radiant water shouts hosanna
My eyes disappear
In jolts
Yes with spasms
Caught by the frankness
Of the wave

The powers of mistakes
Pace on the ground
That lines the two rivers
Narrow wisdom
of the Cossacks
With glowing wounds
Of stained glass

I wait for the scythe
And the beautiful paulownia in my ransacked garden
Surrounds the sky with its musical foliage
Such is the wisdom of shadow
The woman howled
Why hide her breasts
The water would only know how to work
In the absurd
Let me blow on their fine points

De ma bouche aux brindilles de Mongole
Jaillira une pensée sévère
Suis-moi clitoris rauque hérisson rose du désert
Brise tes diadèmes broie tes fiers oiseaux
Je suis tout ce qui reste de ta mère

Je vis alors d'autres personnages
Qui venaient armés de gui et de virgules
Plus dangereux et mutilants
Que maints fusils de guerre
Avide de grands mots la femme chuchota
M'aimes-tu encore
Vois-tu les escadrons de la tradition
Et leurs reliquaires voués aux ossements
De chien
Verseront leurs repas leurs rébus
Leurs Rébecca
Dans la zone interdite
Du cigare

Mais qu'adviendra-t-il de l'expérience matérialiste
Les hommes adossés aux lotus
N'ont que faire de nos épines
Totémiques
De quel coin du néant viendra la fontanelle obscure
De quel obélisque bestial
Tombera le prépuce

L'oeil vague et triste de la mamelle féminine
Doit savoir
J'ai enterré mon image
Yeux ouverts dans la chair
Et la femme sur l'humus

With my mouth of Mongolian twigs
Gushing with a harsh thought
Follow me hoarse clitoris pink hedgehog of the desert
Break your tiaras crush your proud birds
I am all that is left of your mother

I now embody other people
That were armed with mistletoe and commas
More dangerous and mutilating
Than many weapons of war
Eager for big words the woman whispered
Do you still love me
Do you see the death squads of tradition
And their shrines devoted to bones
Of dogs
Will pour their meals their scraps
Their Rebeccas
In the forbidden zone
Of the cigar

But what will become of the materialistic experience
Men backed up against the lotus
Care nothing for our thorns
Totemic
From which corner of the void will the dark fontanelle arrive
From which beastly obelisk
Will the foreskin fall

The sad and dimmed eye of the feminine nipple
Must know
I buried my image
In the open eyes of the flesh
And the woman on the top-soil

Laissa choir
Son masque-éclair
Dans le tombeau de son miroir

À l'Est
Le soleil chemine
Drapé dans les vocables
Inodores
Les offres de reddition
Lance-flammes et travaux d'aiguille
Qui de tout temps décrivent
Dieu

Les deux rives se courbent
Féconde
Je reste là
Fascinée
Le regard fixe le ventre sombre
Maudissant ma grande faim de ton sexe
Verrouillé
Par la famille
Je vois encore
L'escarpement circulaire de ces falaises
Cruelles
Lamentables ruines de combien de devantures
Placées
De l'autre côté de la fièvre
Aussi ne résisterai-je plus
À l'envie
Je finis pourtant par m'endormir
Mon glaïeul éteint
Entre tes quatres dents de devant
Tel le couloir d'un train

Let fall
Her lightning mask
In the grave of her mirror

To the east
The sun ambles
Draped in words
Without smell
The offers of surrender
Flamethrowers and needle work
Who are always describing
God

The two shores are curved
Fertile
I stay there
Fascinated
My look fixed, my stomach gloomy
Cursing my great hunger for your sex
Locked away
By family
I still see
The circular escarpment of the cliffs
Cruel
Pathetic ruins of so many facades
Placed
On the other side of the fever
Also I will no longer resist
The urge
And yet I finally fall asleep
My gladiola turned off
Between four front teeth
Like the corridor of a train

Qui fuit
Tes maigres jambes de rongeur
Augmentent
Mon mal
De mer

Je finis pourtant par m'endormir
Une main dans le seau où grondent les orties
L'autre sur mon pubis aux bornes fluides
Et atermoiements
De fille
Quelle est donc ma patrie
Une ramille jaune dans le fourneau
De ta poitrine
J'aime aussi dit le moine
Le poison le dur hibou
Le demi-aveugle aux pupilles rugueuses
Qui devance le jour binoclé de frais
Louvoyant lentement
Autour de son orbite
L'araignée touffue

Ma route bifurque autour de ton doigt
La moelle tombe
Floconneuse
Sur le blaireau familier
Il fait froid dans l'armoire
Dit la perle
Mon ventre est de cire
Ainsi que mon retard
Sur l'horaire
Un désir vert et clapotant
Tend sa verticale

That flees
Your skinny rodent legs
Increase
My sickness
Of the sea

And yet I finally fall asleep
One hand in the bucket where the nettles growl
The other on my pubis with fluid boundaries
And procrastinations
Of girls
Which one is my country
A small yellow branch in the furnace
Of your chest
I also like it says the monk
The hard poison of the owl
The half-blind with rough pupils
That gets ahead of the glasses
Slowly wavering
Around its orbit
The bushy spider

My path forks around your finger
The marrow falls
Fluffily
On the familiar badger
It's cold in the cupboard
Says the pearl
My stomach is made of wax
So is my lateness
In the schedule
A green lapping desire
Stretches its vertical

Vers la cire
Reconnais regarde cède
Et écoute
L'araignée manger la perle

Ô introuvable son d'une voix lointaine
Dans mille ans tu sauras
Qu'il y a plus de passion
Dans le manchon d'une juive
Que dans les ajours
De la plaine

Je suis la pierre qui pèse entre tes jambes
Pierre souffrant de la végétation
Frôleuse
Pierre de ton signe embrasé
Pierre de ton crâne battu

Je suis le fou-rire de l'occasion perdue
Je suis le fugitif qui court entre les murs
De sa peine
Je suis le cerne de ta vaste clairière
Je suis les barreaux qui meurtrissent ta raison
Je suis la route libre et la chair

Évanouis
Les crampes les ciseaux la maison
Dans la triste rue latérale
De la sonde
Pourquoi tes taches de rousseur
Pâlissent-elle
Mes dents sont inactives
Les vacarme cristallin des ramilles

Towards the wax
Recognize look yield
And listen
To the spider eating the pearl

O unobtainable sound of a distant voice
In a thousand years you will know
That there is more passion
In the muff of a Jewess
Than in the openwork
Of the plain

I am the stone that weighs between your legs
Stone suffering from the greenery
Teasing
Stone of your burning sign
Stone of your beaten skull

I am the giggles of the lost opportunity
I am the fugitive running between the walls
Of his hurt
I am the dark ring of your vast clearing
I am the bars that bruise your reason
I am the free road and the flesh

Fainted
Cramps scissors house
In the sad lateral street
Of the probe
Why do your freckles
Go pale
My teeth are inactive
The crystalline din of small branches

Qui enlacent de leurs tendres injures tes bottes molles
Ne pénètre point le champ clos de ta petite oreille
J'espère que tu souffres
Loin de mon haleine
Et le réseau de tigres
Dans ma main

Que ton buste change d'aspect
Empourpré par la glace
Ta fugue sera ma discipline
Ta coupole mon soleil rougi
Par les morsures
De l'éther

Viens tambouriner dans le creux de mes genoux
La triste réalité de l'heure
Viens prendre possession de mes décorations
De mes fourmis chevalines aux pattes allègres
À l'infime blessure
De blonde
Viens prendre possession de mon suicide
Tu souilleras mon oreiller de tes paroles de lymphe
La publicité
Dilatera tes pupilles
Sans avoir recours à la fellation
Poétique
Sans bannir le sexe du sol
Pourquoi tenir la main du cadavre
Pourquoi souffrir
Le cancer mythique du temps
Passé
Retournera les galets sur la plage inique
Pourquoi chasser la marée au large de la dernière terre

That entwine with their tender injuries your soft boots
Does not enter the arena of your small ear
I hope you are suffering
Far from my breath
And the network of tigers
In my hand

That your bust changes in appearance
Crimson from the ice
Your fugue will be my discipline
Your dome my sun reddened
By the bites
Of the ether

Come drum in the hollow of my knees
The sad reality of the hour
Come take possession of my decorations
Of my horse ants with buoyant feet
To the tiny wound
Of a blonde
Come take possession of my suicide
You will dirty my pillow with your lymph words
The advertising
Will dilate the pupils of your eyes
Without the help of fellatio
Poetic
Without banning the sex from the ground
Why hold the hand of a corpse
Why suffer
The mythical cancer of time
Past
Will overturn the stones on the unjust beach
Why chase the tide off the coast of the last earth

Effacer le contour du grandiose Mexique
Quand dans mon coeur
La vague pulpeuse de l'Orient
Scintille

Un jour je lâcherai la rampe
Et mes jupons coquelicot
Planeront dans le ciel
Comme une terre
J'ai mal
Écumée par la bourrasque
J'entends le chant de ton pipeau
Il glisse sur la lame comme un blessé
Sur la banquise
J'écoute
La douce rumeur de ta langue maudite
Elle vibre dans le sillon
De ma glèbe
J'ai mal
Mais le veilleur passe

Erase the contours of grandiose Mexico
When in my heart
The luscious wave of the Orient
Sparkles

One day I will let go of the handrail
And my poppy skirts
Will glide in the sky
Like an earth
I am in pain
Frothing from the squall
I hear the song of your flute
It slips on the blade like a wounded man
On the ice floe
I am listening
The soft rumor of your cursed tongue
Vibrates in the path
Of my glebe
I am in pain
But the watchman passes by

PANDÉMONIUM

Offre ta gorge à la nuit
Obsédante Afrique
Crache tes dents tes déchets
Tes vertiges
Dans la crème fouettée
De l'église
La trompe de la Mouche à viande
Mince priape ralenti
À l'eau amniotique
Se désaltère
Arrache une pierre du brasier
Une couronne d'épines
Noir vermillon comme les sept lampes
De l'embolie
Riez nomades La vieillesse est casanière
Loin dans la forêt
Un scarabée
Scintille

Seule sur une dune éventée
L'asperge pousse un pointe
Un cri
Le vent le vent aux yeux de perroquet
Aux funèbres processions
Et tournoiements de famine

PANDEMONIUM

Offer your throat to the night
Haunting Africa
Spit your teeth your garbage
Your vertigo
In the whipped cream
Of the church
The trunk of the Meat Fly
Thin priape in decline
Of amniotic water
Quenches his thirst
Rips a stone from the inferno
A crown of thorns
Black vermilion like the seven lamps
Of embolism
Laugh nomads, old age is a homebody
Far in the forest
A beetle
Glimmers

Alone on a windy dune
The asparagus sprouts a tip
A scream
The wind the wind with the eyes of a parrot
With mournful processions
And whirls of starvation

Le vent flagelle tes flancs avides
Tes fœtus de paille
Ta croupe édentée
Frénétique Afrique
Nulle cruauté dans le sang répandu
Nulle contrainte
Afrique grande nuit de la mort édénique
Le regard perlé de l'araignée-loup
Prend naissance dans la tombe
De ton noir gosier sec
Ululez chacals rhombes
Oblations de virginités
Circoncisions
La pluie

La haine aux mains palpitantes
Tambourine sur la peau
De la ténébreuse
Ouganda
Debout
Que tes aisselles flamboient
Que ton sexe batte la campagne
Grise violacée démente de liberté
Ignore les piaillements le cliquetis
De l'oison que l'on excise
Soulève la calotte polaire
Offre le prépuce au couteau
Puis écrasé comme une figue sous le talon urbain
Fais pondre l'épinoche sans sperme déverser
Le végétal
L'arc pointu pas l'ogive
L'arbre phallique
Des sanglots exorbitants comme des bonshommes de neige

The wind whips your greedy flanks
Your straw fetuses
Your toothless croup
Frantic Africa
No cruelty in the spilled blood
No constraints
Africa great night of Edenic death
The pearled gaze of the wolf-spider
Takes root in the tomb
Of your dry black throat
Ululate thundering jackals
Virgin oblations
Circumcisions
Rain

Hate with its pulsating hands
Drums the skin
Of mysterious
Uganda
Stand up
So that your armpits glow
So that your sex travels the countryside
Gray purplish crazy with freedom
Ignore the peeps the clatter
Of the gosling being excised
Lift the polar cap
Offer the foreskin with the knife
Then crushed like a fig under the urban heel
Let the stickleback hatch without semen pour out
The greenery
The pointed arch not the warhead
The phallic tree
Exorbitant sobs like snowmen

Vissent leurs gueules de tromblon
Sur le dos du Têtard
Repos
Matinées luxueuses à la surface du lac enfantin

Sous la coupole et ses volutes
Les avatars et fissions du métal
Souvenir
Sur le tapis diaphane
Rutilant de sang qui s'irise
Les déhanchements d'une langue jamais apprise
Appellent épellent élaborent
L'alphabet du cauchemar
Il faut caresser la gorge de celui que l'on occit
L'arc-boutant du serpent d'airain est visible sous la soie
Offrir son sexe à la nuit

L'étoile du soir
L'androgyne enfin
À cheval sur les deux portes
Errent
Le soleil dans le couchant
La lune à pic dans l'entre-jambes
D'une cathédrale gothique
Miroitent à se fendre l'âme
Dans la boue du chemin faisant
Il faut étouffer le vent d'avant la pluie
Faire taire la chair des voyageurs
La prendre polluée
Sur le crochet du samedi soir
Les rats ailés
Les paradisiers
Verroteries volcaniques

Screw their blunderbuss mouths
On the back of the Tadpole
Rest
Luxurious mornings on the surface of the childish lake

Under the dome and its spirals
The avatars and fission of metal
Memories
On the sheer carpet
Gleaming with iridescent blood
The swagger of a language never learned
Are calling spelling elaboration
The alphabet of nightmares
One must pet the throat of the one we kill
The flying buttress of the bronze snake is visible under silk
To offer one's sex to the night

The night star
Finally the androgynous
Straddling two doors
Wander
The sun inside the sunset
The moon right in the crotch
Of a gothic cathedral
Shimmer to the point of heartbreak
In the mud on the way
One must stifle the wind ahead of the rain
To quiet the flesh of travelers
To take it polluted
On the hook of Saturday night
The winged rats
The birds of paradise
Volcanic beads

Déchets

Les envoûteurs aux gestes larges

Qui sur la face cachée du tombeau

Sèment l'éphélide

Tous planent en hurlant sur le fleuve noir de l'oreille

Placide

Tous Enflés de verdure et lents à vomir

Tous sectaires

Réveillez-vous

Les brises alizées des plages d'Orient sont pommelées à jamais

Le sombre spectacle des cerveaux fuyant par les narines

Ferait rire Gargantua

La bouche pleine

Qu'est la mort après tout

J'éternue

J'ai souvent rêvé de ces rêves

De quais de gare

Le ventre du serpent se gonfle

Il sera mon char

Mille mots imperméables se rallument et pétillent

À fleur de roche

La chicorée folle Plissée et toute frise

Entoure le soleil de ses feuillages intimes

Maladies friselis et dentelures

Ta forme sort de l'ombre

Je reste là Ma tête appuyée sur un vieux battant de songe

Pâteuse désolée

Dans la ouate mouillée des heures mortes

Je n'attends plus qu'une silhouette au fond de l'allée

Cambouis

Qu'un profil au coin de l'œil

Qui irrite et qui dérange

Garbage
Sorcerers with grand gestures
Who on the hidden face of the tomb
Sew the freckle
All glide while howling on the black river of the ear
Placid
All Swollen with greenery and slow to vomit
All sectarian
Wake up
The trade winds of Oriental beaches are forever dappled
The dark spectacle of brains leaking from the nostrils
Would make Gargantua laugh
With his mouth full
What is death after all
I sneeze

I've often dreamt those kind of dreams
Of train stations
The belly of the snake growing
It will be my chariot
A thousand waterproof words reignite and sparkle
On sliver of soil
The crazy chicory Pleated and molded
Surrounds the sun with its intimate foliage
Illnesses shudders and perforations
Your shape emerges from the shadows
I'm staying here My head leaning on an old dream fighter
Pasty apologetic
In the wet padding of the dead hours
I only wait for a silhouette at the end of the alley
Sludge
Just a profile in the corner of the eye
That irritates and bothers

Comme une impression de fumée sur la vitre dépolie
Je n'attends plus que la nuit
La grande marée des scories
La mort océane

Demain l'Afrique
La vie
Entre la poussière et le cri perçant
Le pénis et la campanule
La prunelle du soleil levant saigne sur le sable
Nu
Le train part en arrière
Le ventre tortueux comme une corde tressée
Le sommeil en paliers remontent vers la vallée
C'était demain
L'appel
La hernie qui éclate entre les favoris
De la fortune
Aucun miroir ne saurait voir
La bouche étirée
La grimace amère
L'anus blême des alcooliques
La triste purin de l'aube

Les dents elles-mêmes ne sauraient retenir
Les grandes lèvres
Les glissantes saisons
L'immense bâillement
L'horreur aspirante
Le venin
Le vomi
Le rictus écarlate
La mort tarlatane

Like a smoked impression on the frosted glass
I only wait for the night
The great tide of slag
The ocean death

Tomorrow Africa
Life
Between dust and the piercing scream
The penis and bellflower
The pupil of the rising sun bleeds on the sand
Naked
The train goes backwards
The belly torturous like a woven rope
Sleep in steps rising towards the valley
It was tomorrow
The call
The hernia that bursts between sideburns
Of fortune
No mirror can see
The stretched mouth
The bitter grimace
The pale anus of alcoholics
The sad slurry of dawn

Even teeth wouldn't know how to hold on to
The big lips
The slippery seasons
The gaping yawn
The aspiring horror
The venom
The vomit
The scarlet smirk
The tarlatan death

Mieux vaut baiser des lèvres fanées
Lèvres de toile lèvres de cotonnade
Lèvres sanglantes jamais closes
Mieux vaut fermer la bouche
Qui vomit
Mieux vaut pénétrer la Mère
Sa semence est le mâle désir
Son grand rêve salé
Tari
Mieux vaut mourir en rut
Que renoncer à la luxure
Beau fruit de la révolution
L'homme libre vaincra la mort

Better to kiss wilted lips
Lips of canvas lips of cotton
Bloody lips never closed
Better to close your mouth
That vomits
Better to penetrate the Mother
Her seed is the male desire
His great salty dream
Dwindled
Better to die rutting
Than to give up lust
Beautiful fruit of the revolution
The free man will conquer death

JASMIN D'HIVER

J'avale crie l'anus
L'univers du mensonge
J'avale crie la caverne
Les yeux plombés du mort au petit jour
J'avale hurle la trappe
Les peuples du passé
Enlisés dans la poussière
De la glose
J'avale sanglote l'océan
Les fleuves enflés de viande
Au gré des marées de la guerre
J'avale j'aspire je m'asphyxie
Qui suis-je?
Il suffit de fermer la bouche pour le savoir
La parole incessante du sang sur le trottoir
Le dieu caché sous le tapis troué
De la langue
Buveur de souffrance
Avatar de la maladie
Matinal hirsute
Dieu de la parole errante
Celui qui inverse le cours des années séniles
Celui qui ne craint plus le tourbillon
Ni la haine
Celui qui avale sa queue

WINTER JASMINE

I swallow screams the anus
The universe of lies
I swallow screams the cave
The leaden eyes of the corpse at the break of day
I swallow shrieks the hatch
Peoples of the past
Bogged down with the dust
Of a footnote
I swallow sobs the ocean
The rivers swollen with meat
At the whim of the tides of war
I swallow suck in asphyxiate
Who am I?
You simply need to close your mouth to know
The incessant talk of blood on the sidewalk
The hidden god under the punctured carpet
Of the tongue
Drinker of suffering
Avatar of illness
Shaggy morning
God of wandering talk
Who reverses the course of senile years
Who no longer fears the whirlwind
Or hate
Who swallows his tongue

Chandelle de poix et de soufre allumée
Vilain bouc des montagnes de la lune
Et pourtant Madeleine ne mourut qu'au matin
Blême

À quoi songent les morts
Sous les carreaux noirs et blancs
De la rime enjambée
À quoi songent les noyés
Quand sous les segments de l'alphabet
Ils signent le sable de leurs cheveux mouillés
À quoi songent l'insolent
Qui ne saurait voir la nappe de vie sous la verdure
De l'épitaphe
À quoi songe la cire perdue
D'un visage d'enfant
À la lecture des rides
Sur la surface
De l'étang
Course de nains sur papier blanc
Langage chiffré des oiseaux
Au fil des années du vent
Durée idéale de la nuit derrière les paupières
De celle qui souffre
D'Alexie

Malheur à celui qui étouffe
Le crocodile
Sans perdre son désir d'émeraude
Prenez garde à la tenaille goulue
La dent du jaloux

Candle of pitch and lit sulfur
Ugly goat of the mountains of the moon
And yet Magdalene only died in the morning
Pale

What do dead people dream of
Under the white and black tiles
Of the arched rhyme
What do drowned people dream of
When under parts of the alphabet
They sign the sand with their wet hair
What does the insolent man dream of
Who can't see the layer of life under the greenery
Of the epitaph
What does the lost wax
Of a child's face dream of
To the reading of wrinkles
On the surface
Of the marsh
Race of dwarves on white paper
Numbered language of the birds
Over the years of wind
Perfect length of the night behind the eyelids
Of the woman who suffers
Of Alexie

Woe to him who chokes
The crocodile
Without losing their emerald desire
Be careful of the greedy pincers
The jealous tooth

Est en deuil
Malheur à celui qui étreint
Le manche et non l'épieu
Il sera fécondé par la lance qui saigne
Et les hommes recroquevillés dans le ventre de la falaise
Mourront sans revoir le renard pâle
Tout le monde ne saurait être forgeron
En pays Dogon en pays Dogon
C'est pourquoi le cadavre pourrit

On voudrait s'arrêter
Être la trop visible épouse
De l'orient vermeil
Gorgée de terre comme l'été
Au bord du Nil
Prendre le chemin qui s'éloigne
Si tu me parlais doux
Le rongeur implacable laissera son ombre nue
On voudrait s'arrêter
Voir la pluie dénuder la plaine
Être deux morts dans la forêt
De la tombe

Apparition forcée
Quatre hautes statues
Toujours les mêmes malgré la verdure
Gardiens posthumes du phallus de pierre
Le dur désir silencieux
Celui qui vrille les entrechats
Sous les draps mouillés
De la mousson

Is mourning
Woe to him who grasps
The sleeve and not the stake
He will be fertilized by the bleeding lance
And the men curled up in the belly of the cliff
Will die without seeing the pale fox
Not everyone can be a blacksmith
In Dogon country in Dogon country
It's why the corpse rots

We'd like to stop
To be the overly noticed wife
Of the vermeil orient
Stuffed with soil like summer
On the shores of the Nile
To take the path that recedes
If you spoke softly to me
The relentless rodent will leave its naked shadow
We'd like to stop
To see the rain strip the plain
To be two corpses in the forest
Of the tomb

Forced appearance
Four high statues
Always the same despite the greenery
Posthumous guardians of the stone phallus
The hard silent desire
The one that twists the entrechats
Under the wet sheets
Of the monsoon

Reconnu le taureau accroupi dans la fange
Les chien errants les mendiants
Le grand doute haletant
L'illusion que cela bouge
Dans l'angle sec de l'œil
Tout est là inscrit sur les murs blancs flottants
Il faut tuer l'ancêtre dans l'œuf
Car dès le commencement
Rien n'est

Un remède à la mélancolie
Un dimanche de janvier
Chargé d'épices et de boue
Comme le cadavre prisonnier de son savoir-mourir
Qui aspire sans mâchoire à dire son dernier mot
Le grand rire congelé d'un sandwich au jambon
Ou la conversation des sourds attachés par les poignets
À l'anneau de la solitude
Et les parades carnassières du vieux démon de minuit
Ne changeront rien à l'affaire
L'angoisse se contracte aux limites de ce qui n'est pas
Engeance de chacal
Elle, assise sur le lit
Comme la nuit sur la dune
Pleure et dit au petit jour
J'ai envie de rendre

L'odeur de la poussière
Dans une bouche automnale
Morte après la mort du soleil
Masque de cendres sur des visages vermillon

Recognized the bull crouching in the mire
The wandering dogs the beggars
The great panting doubt
The illusion that it moves
In the sharp corner of the eye
Everything is there written on the white floating walls
One must kill the forefathers in the egg
Because from the beginning
Nothing is

A cure for melancholy
A Sunday in January
Loaded with spices and mud
Like the corpse captive of his death know-how
That strives without the jaw to say his final word
The great laugh frozen in a ham sandwich
Where the conversation of the deaf tied at the wrists
To the ring of solitude
And the carnivorous parades of the old demon of midnight
Will change nothing
The anguish shrinks at the limits of that which is not
Scum of jackals
She, sitting on the bed
Like the night on a dune
Cries and tells the breaking day
I feel sick

The smell of dust
In an autumnal mouth
Dead after the death of the sun
Mask of ashes on vermilion faces

Souvenir de la Grèce
Derrière les volets des grands vieillards
Couvent
Leurs racines spongieuses sur un lit de pierraille
Autant de théories condamnées au silence
Je saluai un cheval qui passa son chemin
Pourquoi l'eau toujours l'eau
Entre la terreur et l'éveil
Qui a ouvert la bouche de l'homme

Vénus petite lune
Maladie de la fange vénéneuse
Aux tétons de potence
Aux pieds palmés rabougris
Par sa trop longue station debout
Un geste de la pipe
Dans la jungle des ténèbres
Et la verge de la vierge vire au vert vertigo
Vertiges

Vénus virago archaïque
Racine flottante sur la rade foraine
Celle qui panse les tonsurés furtifs
Celle qui défèque dans la souricière
Atavique
Celle qui se vautre celle qui s'accroupit
Sur le cumulo-volcan lieu de la crémation
Du mouton sous hypnose
Vénus vile acrobate des feux de bivouac
Celle qui cisaille le ciel de ses cuisses carnivores
Celle qui dérive sur les vastes pistes de Nazsca
Viscères noués vrombissement sévères

Memories of Greece
Behind the shutters of great old men
Smoldering
Their spongy roots on a bed of rubble
So many theories condemned to silence
I greet a horse who went his own way
Why water always water
Between terror and awakening
Who has opened the mouth of man

Venus the little moon
Disease of the venomous mire
With nipples of gallows
With stunted webbed feet
By her lengthy time standing
A gesture from the pipe
In the jungle of darkness
And the virgin's shaft shifts to vertiginous green
Vertigo

Venus archaic virago
Floating root in the harbor fairgrounds
She who bandages those furtive people with shaved heads
She who defecates in the mousetrap
Atavistic
She who wallows she who crouches
On the cumulo-volcano place of cremation
Of the hypnotized sheep
Venus vile acrobat of bivouac fires
She who prunes the sky with her carnivorous thighs
She who drifts on the vast lines of Nazca
Knotted viscera severe roar

Répandant la soupe virevoltante d'une nuit de solitude
Dans l'écuelle du chien
Il vomit
Heureux les calcinés de l'Inde
Par-delà le ravin ils découvrent
Les à-pics de l'éternel retour

Spreading the twirling soup from a night of solitude
In the dog's bowl
He vomits
Joyful the scorched of India
Beyond the ravine they discover
The sheer cliffs of the eternal return

Ne jamais dire son rêve
A celui qui ne vous aime pas
L'oreille hostile est tarie
La bouche amère calomnie
La haine vomit le sable du sablier
Plus vite toujours plus vite
La nuit trahie avorte
Une passion au présent déjà passée
Et la peur ne fait qu'augmenter
La rage du caïman
La taille du cancer
Enfouissez vos rêves dans les poches sous vos yeux
Ils seront à l'abri de l'envie
Ils seront à l'abri de l'adage
Qui veux que l'Africain babille
Et que tous les vieux soient sages

Never share your dream
With the one who doesn't love you
The cruel ear has dried out
The soured mouth slurs
Hate vomits the sand of the hourglass
Faster always faster
The betrayed night aborts
A passion whose present has already passed
And fear only heightens
The rage of the caiman
The size of the cancer
Stuff your dreams into the bags under your eyes
They will be hidden from envy
They will be hidden from the old saying
That claims the African babbles
And all the old are wise

Les eaux de ce pays-là ne s'écoulent jamais
Les marins ne craignent point la tempête

Les femmes n'entament plus les rondes de l'enfance
Leurs maisons dissonantes voguent autant que des navires
Aveugles elles plongent sous la neige
Aveugles elles rejaillissent dans l'écume du printemps
Confondant le temps qu'il fait avec le temps qui passe
Mais le nid si parfaitement circonscrit s'asphyxie
La pluie et les beaux draps couvent des oeufs de serpent

Laissez toute espérance le vent du Nord s'est tu
Les yeux blancs de l'oubli sont fixes à tout jamais
Et l'inconnu ne reviendra plus de l'exil

The waters of that country never flow
The sailors never fear the storm

The women no longer initiate the dances of childhood
Their dissonant homes drift as much as their ships
Blind they dive under the snow
Blind they spill back into the springtime surf
Confusing the weather with passing time
But the perfectly circumscribed nest asphyxiates
The rain and good sheets sit on the eggs of the serpent

Let go of all hope the Northern wind is quiet
The white eyes of oblivion are set forever
And the stranger will never return from exile

Brûler de l'encens dans la quiétude d'une chambre
Loin derrière les récifs d'une journée chaotique

Suivre de longues queues de noir vêtues
Dans les cimetières où dorment les années révolues

Pleurer des morts qui fleurissent comme jambons de Parme

Creuser des rides dans les champs

Crever l'oeil stagnant de la nuit

Embrasser le pied d'un pape alpiniste
Ou laper l'huile qui suinte des idoles endolories
Par trop de caresses

Tout cela me fatigue
M'exaspère

Rien ne vaut une bonne dose de rage
Pour partir
Car le pied crée le chemin use le roc
Et renverse le totem qui titube
Dans la peur tropicale des églises

To burn incense in the quiet of a room
Far behind the reefs of a chaotic day

To follow long tails dressed in black
In the graveyard where sleep the bygone years

To mourn the dead who bloom like Parma hams

To dig the wrinkles in the fields

To pierce the stagnant eye of the night

To embrace the foot of an alpinist pope
Or lap the oil that oozes from the idols sore
From too much stroking

All this tires me out
Exasperates me

Nothing beats a good dose of rage
When leaving
Because the foot makes the path wears the rock down
And knocks over the totem that teeters
In the tropical fear of the churches

Il faut noyer le coq à sa naissance
Empêcher les aveugles de mener le train

Les prairies de la mort papillonnantes de papiers gras
Bordent nos songes de leurs hauts cris
Raison de plus pour en rire

One must drown the rooster at birth
Prevent the blind from leading the train

The prairies of death fluttering with greasy papers
Line our dreams with their high screams
All the more reason to laugh about it

TROUS NOIRS

Nommer une blessure
avant qu'elle ne suppure
Partout l'objet du mépris
saigne et pustule
à bon escient
Nommer l'infamie rose sous ses dentelles
avant qu'elle n'impose
Partout l'homme se met à genoux
pleure et transpire
flétri par le deuil solitaire
Partout le malaise fleurit
L'empire du cadavre s'étend
Nommer une fosse une fois recouverte
semer dessus des glands
et passez votre chemin
car la mort est contagieuse
et son nom souillera vos lèvres
vos lèvres votre langue votre bouche
votre blessure

Dans un monde tout gris
Une femme étouffée dans sa graisse
Crie sa solitude
Deux mains crépitent

BLACK HOLES

To name a wound
before it festers
Everywhere the object of contempt
bleeds and blisters
deliberately
To name the pink infamy under her lacework
before she imposes
Everywhere man takes a knee
cries and sweats
withered by the solitary grief
Everywhere uneasiness blooms
The empire of the corpse spreads
To name a grave once it's covered
to sew acorns on it
and go on your way
because death is contagious
and her name will soil your lips
your lips your tongue your mouth
your wound

In an all grey world
A woman choked by her flesh
Screams her loneliness
Two hands crackle

Dans un miroir d'encre
Une bouche pleine de viande
Blasphème et vocifère
La mayonnaise tourne
Et brouille les vitres
L'or et la tempête
Grondent au-dehors
La femme mange pour se faire connaître
Et meurt la bouche ouverte
Devant le sexe en érection
D'un veilleur de nuit
Dernier soubresaut de la boulimie

La porte est fermée de l'intérieur
Je suis en retard d'une heure
De maigres voiliers se rangent le long des murs
Leurs ancres au repos
Leurs voiles endeuillées
Un gros doigt se prélasse sur un canapé
D'un fusain léger il trace les contours d'un visage féminin
Signes de la virginité autres que l'hymen
Je suis hantéee par les lambeaux absurdes
D'une phrase à peine entendue
Primitive épellation dans la nuit du temps perdu

L'angoisse tient le cœur
de sa petite main de fer
Dans le ventre de la géante la boue
s'agite
L'homme à tête de crocodile
mastic les boyaux

In an ink mirror
A mouth full of meat
Curses and screams
The mayonnaise sours
And blurs the windows
The gold and the storm
Thunder outside
The woman eats to make herself known
And dies with her mouth open
In front of the erect sex
Of a night warden
Last upheaval of bulimia

The door is locked from the inside
I'm an hour late
Thin sailboats line up along the walls
Their anchors at rest
Their sails in mourning
A fat finger basks on the sofa
With a light charcoal he draws the outline of a feminine face
Signs of virginity other than the hymen
I am haunted by the absurd shreds
Of a scarcely heard phrase
Primitive spelling in the night of lost time

Anguish holds the heart
with its small iron hand
In the belly of the giant the mud
tosses and turns
The man with a crocodile head
chews the bowels

de la grappe
humaine
Des vers noirs s'éprennent
Des vers blancs gravés de chair
font des bulles
Où sont les vieillards de mer?

Qu'il te souvienne
l'heure du soir
où nageaient au loin
les îles riantes
de notre amour
Qu'il te souvienne
le chien blanc
les yeux crayeux
le mufle flamand
assoiffé de puissance
sous le pansement de sa peur
Qu'il te souvienne
les perles du soleil
jetées sur le sable
comme autant de fosses profondes
dans la graisse douloureuse
de la chair coupée
Qu'il te souvienne
hélas mon amour hélas
de l'entour de ces murailles
où murmure la bouche écumeuse
de la belle morte ensevelie
Qu'il te souvienne
l'enchaînement des horreurs
de la nuit

of the human
vine
Black worms fall in love
White worms stuffed with flesh
make bubbles
Where are the old men of the sea?

May he remind you
of the evening hour
where swam in the distance
islands laughing
of our love
May he remind you
of the white dog
the chalky eyes
the Flemish muzzle
thirsting for power
under the bandaid of fear
May he remind you
of the pearls of the sun
thrown on the sand
like so many deep pits
in the painful fat
of sliced flesh
May he remind you
alas my love alas
of the surroundings of these walls
where whispers the frothy mouth
of the beautiful buried death
May he remind you
of the sequence of horrors
of the night

Le monde est un oiseau
Il tape des pieds
Sur une tombe ouverte
Il picore le crâne d'un enfant
Mou sous son bec d'acier
Il bat des ailes
Il chante
Le monde est un oiseau qui chie

Tombés du soleil sur le rivage où
nulle barque est amarrée
ceux qui pensaient mériter le ciel
virent clairement passer sur sa roue enflammée
un homme à tête de crapaud
La prudence exige de ne jamais laisser séjourner
l'ordure à la surface du sol
Une houle de sang et de fiente
gronde bave et revient
s'abattre sur la terre poudreuse de mort
Les voyageurs furent battus et ils perdirent leurs visages
Piétinés par un bousier géant roi de la peur gelée
L'homme à tête de crapaud roula sa roue grinçante
comme un vieille verrue
dans le trou noir spiralé de sa tombe
Un grand fracas de sabots brise la marmite
Un centaure déchiqueté comme une ombre
au coin du jour
aspire la sanie des cadavres pour nourrir sa progéniteur
Le nœud du mariage serre le cou du cavalier
"À mort" hurlent les moines
écartant les jambes du cheval éventré
accolant leurs lèvres à ses plaies

The world is a bird
It stomps its feet
On an open grave
It pecks the skull of a child
Soft under the steel beak
It flaps its wings
It sings
The world is a shitting bird

Fallen from the sun on the shore where
no boat has moored
those who thought they deserved the sky
saw passing by on its swollen wheel
a man with the head of a toad
Caution requires to never allow
filth on the surface of soil
A swell of blood and droppings
thunders drools and returns
to descend on the earth powdery with death
The travelers were beaten and they lost their faces
Trampled by an enormous beetle giant king of frozen fear
The man with the head of a toad rolled his squeaky wheel
like an old wart
in the black spiral hole of his tomb
A large crash of hooves breaks the pot
A centaur shredded like a shadow
in the day's corner
breathes in the pus of the corpses to feed his progeny
The tie of marriage strangles the horseman
"To the death" scream the monks
spreading the legs of the gutted horse
pressing their lips to his wounds

il pompent le sang du cheval et du cavalier
pour couler eux-mêmes liquides
vers quelle glotte obscure?
Un batelier fou tente de gagner le large
sur sa barque abritée de suaires en pavois
mais déjà les êtres anxieux des profondeurs
lèvent la tête
leurs yeux sans paupières comme pondus
sur un amas de lamproies
blanches scories de la nuit gélatine
demandant leur dû de toutes leurs bouches suceuses
et le batelier quittant son banc
tombe dans la vase déferlante
du bateau de la vie il préféra la lame
Au loin errent des créatures fanées
mollement déformées dans leur étau placentaire
victimes de l'immense mâchoire qui galope sur la plage
gluante de ganglions entassés
"L'hygiène est satisfaisante" brame-t-elle
arrachant les capons flasques de leur cachot
"Connaître c'est aimer" répond le crapaud sur sa roue translucide
tournant sur l'espace courbe d'une narine échancrée
attendant l'aube du matin qui ne poindra
plus jamais

La foule attendait sur la place
Le vent broutait l'herbe brin à brin
Une obscurité hostile étouffait les bêtes sauvages
Les grands arbres bégayaient de toutes leurs langues feuillues
La foule attendant sans sourciller
L'arrivée de l'insecte géant accourant enfin aux vivres
Jouant des pattes

they pump the blood of the horse and horseman
to flow liquid themselves
towards which obscure glottis?
A mad boatman tries to reach the open sea
on his boat sheltered with bulwark shrouds
but already the anguished beings of the depths
lift their heads
their eyes without lids as though laid
on a cluster of lampreys
white slags of the gelatinous night
demanding their dues with their sucker mouths
and the boatman leaving his bench
falls in the surging slime
of the boat of life he preferred the blade
Far away wander faded creatures
softly deformed in their placental noose
victims of the giant jaw that gallops on the beach
slimy with piled up ganglions
"Hygiene is satisfied" she bellows
ripping the limp cowards from their dungeon
"To know is to love" answers the toad on his translucid wheel
Turning on the curved line of an indented nostril
waiting for the dawn of the morning that will break
never again

The crowd waited on-site
The wind grazed the grass blade by blade
A hostile darkness choked the wild beasts
The large trees stuttered in all their leafy tongues
The crowd waited without batting an eye
The arrival of the giant insect running up to the food supplies
Getting in the way

Poussant du dos
Minaudant dans sa mince gaine cylindrique
Prêt à engloutir de ses grandes lèvres difformes
La nourriture faisandée
Des hommes
La foule attendait
Amas confus de membres disjoints
La bousier géant et sa besogne ordurière
La foule attendait
Le vent bruissait dans les haillons de la forêt
Et le cauchemar voluptueux
Recourbait fortement
Les abdomens
Humides
Piteuse clôtures dites-vous?
Tel est le destin de la foule

Écoute
le cris des courlis dans les roseaux
près de la mer
L'ombre passe sur la campagne
comme une main sur un visage lisse
Qui fermera les yeux de celle qui se meurt
dans l'écume des coteaux bleus
Les ramiers roucoulants de l'agonie
entourent le haut rocher de la solitude
Elle lutte contre l'asphyxie. La terreur
comme l'insecte tapi sous l'écorce d'un arbre en feu
Écoute le cri des courlis dans les roseaux
c'est peut-être la mort qui passe

Prodding
Simpering in his thin circular sheath
Ready to swallow with his large deformed lips
The gamey food
Of men
The crowd waited
Confused pile of disjointed limbs
The giant beetle and his dirty work
The crowd waited
The wind rustled in the rags of the forest
And the curvaceous nightmare
Strongly bent
The abdomens
Wet
Pitiful ending you say?
Such is the fate of the crowd

Listen
the cries of curlews in the reeds
near the sea
The shadow passes over the countryside
like a hand on a smooth face
That will close the eyes of she who is dying
in the surf of the blue hillside
The wood pigeons cooing in agony
surround the top of the rock of solitude
She fights asphyxia. Terror
like an insect hidden away under the bark of a tree on fire
Listen to the cry of the curlew in the reeds
It is perhaps death passing by

Ne faut-il pas être fou
À tout âge
De porter sa frayeur
Comme un masque de craie
Sur son visage
La bouche ouverte sur un cri
Les yeux blancs eux aussi
Ne faut-il pas être fou
Sous l'orage
De porter un fruit dans l'ornière
De son ventre
Plus âpre qu'un abcès
Plus avide que l'absence
Un fruit plus nocif
Que la nuit
Plus pulpeux que la mort
Prêt à éclater prêt à exploser
Un fruit sans pépins
Fort de sa boulimie
Fruit maudit de la peur
Lubrique
Banquise

Un rideau d'anxiété s'enroule autour de ses jambes
L'angoisse loge dans son nombril
Ce tiroir matelassé à demi ouvert
L'homme cabré au-dessus d'une femme
Ainsi que le bâton à tête de cheval des anciens mimes
Flotte au-dessus d'une mare
L'homme essaie de conjurer les petits objets aux contours irréguliers
Qui envahissent sa gorge
Et l'empêchent d'avaler

Must we not be mad
At any age
To carry our fear
Like a chalk mask
On our face
Mouth open on a scream
White eyes as well
Must we not be mad
Under the thunderstorm
To bear fruit in the rut
Of our belly
Harsher than an abscess
Hungrier than an absence
A more harmful fruit
Than the night
More fleshy than death
Ready to burst ready to explode
A fruit without seeds
Confident in its bulimia
Cursed fruit of fear
Lustful
Ice field

A curtain of angst curls around her legs
The angst stays in her bellybutton
This quilted drawer half open
A man prancing on top of a woman
As well as the stick with a horse's head of the ancient mimes
Floats on top of a pond
The man tries to conjure little things with irregular shapes
That invade his throat
And prevent him from swallowing

Du sang tombe de ses yeux
Comme les premières gouttes lentes
D'une lourde pluie d'été
Il jouit
Une trace sinueuse sur le parquet
Il gît
Un grand poids pèse sur son visage
La femme se démène pour cueillir son dernier souffle
Dans un sac de soie sauvage
Les cymbales et les tambours se sont tus
Qui va se marier?

Faut-il respirer la mort pour guérir son esprit
L'érable sculpte le vent
Sans couteau
J'attends le tournant de la roue
Bouche sèche d'insomnie
Ravie de peur
On abat des arbres dans mon cœur
Un pesant fœtus
Surgit des rafales de la nuit
L'humilité glissante du têtard
M'écœure
Belle et sinistre promiscuité
Le vent bouge dans le miroir
J'ai le corps pourri dans la terre
Il est presque trop tard
Pour se réveiller

On ne vit pas avec les morts
Ils glissent sur le tapis roulant de l'oubli

Blood falls from his eyes
Like the first slow drops
Of a heavy summer rain
He comes here
A sinuous mark launches on the floor
He lies there
A large load weighs down his face
A woman scrambles to pluck her last breath
In a bag of wild silk
The cymbals and drums have gone quiet
Who will get married?

Must one breathe death to heal one's spirit?
The maple sculpts the wind
Without a knife
I wait for the turn of the wheel
Dry mouth of insomnia
Delighted with fear
The trees in my heart are being slaughtered
A heavy fetus
Appears from the gusts of the night
The slippery humility of the tadpole
Sickens me
Beautiful and sinister promiscuity
The wind moves in the mirror
My body is rotten in the earth
It's almost too late
To waken

We don't live with the dead
They slip on the treadmill of oblivion

Vers quels noirs pâturages
Ils flottent et tremblent dans le vent du soir
Leurs yeux se vident comme une baignoire
Leurs sexes atrophiés pendent
Entre leurs jambes enlisées
Dans la boue du souvenir
On ne vit pas avec les morts
Leurs bouches pleines de ouate
Rient de nos vains efforts
Leurs soupirs affamés déchirent l'air
Nous nous sommes aimés.
Mais ils ne se souviennent guère
Tout occupés comme ils sont
À jouir de leur deuil
Caracolant sur l'abîme
Comme chevaux de frise
Heureux dans l'horreur
Les morts passent leur chemin
Débonnaires et la tête vide

Towards what dark pastures
They float and tremble in the evening wind
Their eyes are emptied like bathtubs
Their atrophied genitals hang
Between their legs bogged down
In the mud of memories
We don't live with the dead
Their mouths full of cotton padding
Laugh of our vain efforts
Their hungry sighs shred the air
We loved each other.
But they don't remember
Busy like they are
Taking pleasure in their mourning
Prancing on the abyss
Like a Frisian horse
Happy in horror
The dead go on their way
Good natured and empty headed

Joyce Mansour was born in England in 1928 to a Jewish family of Syrian descent who moved to Egypt when she was still an infant. She grew up among the English-speaking elite of Egypt. Despite her privileged childhood, she was deeply scarred by the loss of her mother to cancer at 15 years old and the death of her first husband six months into their marriage, when she was just 18. She learned to speak and write in French when she married her second husband, a Francophone Egyptian, and was exiled to Paris when Nasser came to power. Mansour was part of the inner circle of Surrealists, a close friend of André Breton, and the most significant poet to join the group after World War II. She wrote 16 books of poetry, as well as prose works and plays. She lived in Paris, France until her death in 1986 at age of 58.